The Price of Dominance

The New Weapons of Mass Destruction and Their Challenge to American Leadership

Jan Lodal

COUNCIL ON FOREIGN RELATIONS PRESS
NEW YORK

The Council on Foreign Relations, Inc., a nonprofit, nonpartisan national organization founded in 1921, is dedicated to promoting understanding of international affairs through the free and civil exchange of ideas. The Council's members are dedicated to the belief that America's peace and prosperity are firmly linked to that of the world. From this flows the mission of the Council: to foster America's understanding of other nations—their peoples, cultures, histories, hopes, quarrels, and ambitions—and thus to serve our nation through study and debate, private and public.

From time to time, books, monographs, reports, and papers written by members of the Council's research staff or others are published as a "Council on Foreign Relations Publication."

THE COUNCIL TAKES NO INSTITUTIONAL POSITION ON POLICY ISSUES AND HAS NO AFFILIATION WITH THE U.S. GOVERNMENT. ALL STATEMENTS OF FACT AND EXPRESSIONS OF OPINION CONTAINED IN ALL ITS PUBLICATIONS ARE THE SOLE RESPONSIBILITY OF THE AUTHOR OR AUTHORS.

Council on Foreign Relations books are distributed by Brookings Institution Press (1-800-275-1447). For further information about the Council or this book, please write the Council on Foreign Relations, 58 East 68th Street, New York, NY 10021, or call the Director of Communications at (212) 434-9400. Visit our website at www.cfr.org.

Library of Congress Cataloging-in-Publication Data

Lodal, Jan, 1943–
  The price of dominance: the new weapons of mass destruction
and their challenge to American leadership / by Jan Lodal.
      p.   cm.
  ISBN 0-87609-274-1 (pbk.)
  1. Arms control. 2. United States—Foreign relations. 3. United
States—Military policy. I. Title.
  JZ5625 .L63 2001
  327.1'745'0973—dc21
                            00-065604

COUNCIL ON FOREIGN RELATIONS

58 EAST 68TH STREET • NEW YORK • NEW YORK 10021
Tel 212 434 9400 *Fax* 212 434 9880

Leslie H. Gelb
President

Dear Colleague:

I am pleased to send you a copy of the Council's newest publication, *The Price of Dominance: The New Weapons of Mass Destruction and Their Challenge to American Leadership*, by Council member Jan Lodal.

Despite the demise of the Cold War nuclear standoff, weapons of mass destruction continue to pose serious challenges to the United States in new and ever more complex ways. In this book, Jan has undertaken the monumental task of writing a cogent analysis of these new threats and suggests policies the new Bush administration should implement to adequately deal with these issues.

We trust this analysis will contribute to a wider debate and understanding of the security and diplomatic challenges facing the United States.

Leslie H. Gelb

Leslie H. Gelb

The Price
of Dominance

Contents

List of Acronyms

ABM	Antiballistic Missile
BMD	Ballistic Missile Defense
BWC	Biological Weapons Convention
CBW	Chemical and Biological Weapons
CTBT	Comprehensive Test Ban Treaty
CTR	Cooperative Threat Reduction
CWC	Chemical Weapons Convention
EKV	Exoatmospheric Kill Vehicle
GPALS	Global Protection Against Limited Strikes
HUMINT	Human Intelligence
IAEA	International Atomic Energy Agency
ICBM	Intercontinental Ballistic Missile
IFF	Identification Friend-or-Foe
INF	Intermediate-Range Nuclear Forces
LECO	Law Enforcement Cooperation Officer
MAD	Mutual Assured Destruction
MEADS	Medium Extended Air Defense System
MIRV	Multiple Independently Targetable Reentry Vehicles
MTCR	Missile Technology Control Regime

NMD	National Missile Defense
NPT	Nuclear Nonproliferation Treaty
NRRC	Nuclear Risk Reduction Centers
NSA	National Security Agency
OPCW	Office for the Prevention of Chemical Weapons
PAC	Patriot Advanced Capability
SALT	Strategic Arms Limitation Treaty
SDI	Strategic Defense Initiative
SIOP	Single Integrated Operations Plan
SLBM	Submarine Launched Ballistic Missile
SSBM	Surface-to-Surface Ballistic Missile
SSBN	Nuclear Powered Ballistic Missile Submarine (Trident)
SSP	Stockpile Stewardship Program
START	Strategic Arms Reduction Treaty
STRANSS	Strategic Transparency, Safety, and Stability Treaty
TBM	Theater Ballistic Missiles
THAAD	Theater High-Altitude Area Defense System
TMD	Theater Missile Defense
UNSCOM	United Nations Special Commission on Iraq
WMD	Weapon(s) of Mass Destruction

Foreword

The nuclear standoff between the Soviet Union and the United States is over, but weapons of mass destruction (WMD) remain the most serious threat to the security of the United States. The Information Revolution has spread the knowledge needed to develop these weapons and driven the globalization of commerce that makes export controls on them harder to enforce each year. As a result, nuclear, chemical, and biological weapons are increasingly the means by which rogue states and terrorist organizations may choose to oppose the United States. At the same time, China and Russia, even though they are no longer America's enemies, retain large nuclear forces that pose a potential threat.

In this book, Jan Lodal, a former senior official responsible for arms control and defense policy in both Republican and Democratic administrations, makes an intriguing case that the new WMD challenge is an inevitable result of America's military, political, cultural, and economic dominance. Throughout history, nation-states have coalesced to oppose hegemonic powers, even those with apparently benign intentions. Lodal identifies important changes that can be made in U.S. strategic policy to ameliorate the opposition of other powers to American-led efforts against WMD proliferation. In particular, he strongly urges abandoning the Cold War nuclear doctrine of "damage limiting" and its resulting "prompt retaliatory" nuclear attack plans. Dropping these plans would permit reducing U.S. nuclear forces to 1,200 weapons from today's total of almost 10,000, without abandoning any important aspects of nuclear doctrine. If the United States eventually deploys "light" antiballistic missile defenses (which Lodal favors and both political parties now seem to support), failing to abandon the "prompt retaliatory" war plans would give the United States a de facto first-strike capability and absolute military dominance over all other nations combined. In such circumstances, it would be impossible to organize the tight cooperation of other states, particularly of Russia, China, and France, that is so absolutely necessary to stop the new WMD threats.

The Price of Dominance offers an integrated program for moving away from the Cold War approach that still dominates U.S. WMD policy to one aimed at achieving multinational cooperation against WMD threats while retaining nuclear deterrence as the bedrock of America's security policy. The Lodal program begins with a new nuclear strategy that reaffirms deterrence of Russia and the "nuclear umbrella" over friends and allies, along with four very limited "first-use" nuclear missions. But it explicitly renounces any first-strike capability against Russia and the forces and war plans supporting a first-strike capability. The new strategy would include limited missions for ballistic missile defenses. America would use its unilateral changes in nuclear strategy and forces to forge an international consensus accepting limited national ballistic missile defenses as enhancements rather than threats to strategic stability. Nuclear arms control would continue to play an important role but would be restructured from the Cold War Strategic Arms Reduction and Antiballistic Missile treaties to a new Strategic Transparency, Safety, and Stability treaty (STRANSS).

In the context of these changes, it should be possible to greatly enhance the acceptance and enforcement of the three treaties that prohibit the proliferation of WMD—the Nuclear Nonproliferation Treaty, the Chemical Weapons Convention, and the Biological Weapons Convention. Lodal argues that the role of law enforcement, both domestic and multinational, will have to be increased at the expense of reliance on multilateral enforcement organizations such as the Office for the Prevention of Chemical Weapons and the International Atomic Energy Agency. The dismal experience of the United States Special Commission in enforcing arms control in Saddam Hussein's Iraq illustrates the severe limits to the effectiveness of U.N.-based enforcement organizations. In the end, Lodal argues that the traditional tools of diplomacy, sanctions, and military force will have to be used to enforce nonproliferation.

The Price of Dominance proposes a strategic vision of strong deterrence coupled with open international cooperation around which the new president could organize a U.S. policy toward WMD that could develop wide support domestically and internationally. Without a new vision, the gridlock that has characterized arms control, antiballistic missile defense policy, and strategic relations with Russia, China, and France will continue. What intrigues me about Jan Lodal's book is its bold moves and coherent vision, so essential in any effort to combat the extremism, terrorism, and anarchy that drive the new WMD threats.

Leslie H. Gelb
President
Council on Foreign Relations

Preface

This book grew out of the work of a Council on Foreign Relations study group formed in 1999 to assess the future of arms control. The Comprehensive Test Ban Treaty (CTBT) had been rejected by the U.S. Senate, and Russia had refused to ratify the second Strategic Arms Reduction Treaty (START). It seemed that arms control efforts had come to a halt; a completely new approach would be needed to break the gridlock.

In the summer of 1999, the Clinton administration acquiesced to long-standing pressure from Republicans in the U.S. Senate to announce a tentative deployment date for a national missile defense. The proximate cause of the new policy was North Korea's test of a long-range rocket. The Antiballistic Missile (ABM) decision added greatly to the sense that the arms control approach built up since the Eisenhower administration had come to an end. The United States insisted on modifying the ABM Treaty to permit deploying the defense against North Korea, and Russia insisted on keeping the treaty intact. Both sides threatened to withdraw from the arms control regime if the other refused to budge.

As I compiled the results of our study group discussions in the fall of 1999, I came to conclude that the gridlock in arms control could not simply be blamed on bad negotiating tactics, turbulence in Russian politics, opposition from Senator Jesse Helms (R.-N.C.), or America's refusal to ratify the CTBT. All of these were factors to be dealt with, to be sure. But the problems in arms control were symptoms of a more fundamental challenge to American foreign policy. The United States had not completed the shift from a policy based on the bipolar balance of the Cold War to one based on America's growing dominance in world affairs.

Most nations accept the benign nature of American intentions and the moral strength of our political system and culture. But in the end, they will assess their positions based on our capabilities, not our intentions. They know that an America with absolute military dominance over all other powers could all too easily fall under the control of political forces that would insist on using that dominance to impose America's political, economic, and cultural system on the rest of the world. They will thus oppose American power, even if it means taking serious risks to their own societies by permitting the proliferation of new weapons of mass destruction and maintaining larger nuclear and other military forces than they can afford or need for their immediate defense.

The U.S. failure to complete the transition away from the bipolar Cold War world led me to conclude that only a new, integrated, comprehensive approach to the challenge of new weapons of mass destruction could be effective. It would have to encompass not only arms control, but a new nuclear strategy and force posture, a new approach to antiballistic missile defenses, better enforcement of the existing chemical, biological, and nuclear nonproliferation regimes, and a major enhancement of law enforcement and intelligence capabilities (including dramatically increased international cooperation). Most significantly, the new president would have to articulate a strategic vision consistent with the strong international cooperation absolutely necessary to meet the challenge of the proliferation of weapons of mass destruction. Thus, a book that started out to focus on arms control ended up focusing on these broader issues, but with arms control, including both its history and its future, being the major sub-theme. The book is short by design; I avoided the temptation to elaborate many important details in order to give the main strategic themes more prominence. The details of a new program and policy will in any case have to emerge out of negotiations within the leadership of the next administration, between the executive and congressional branches, and with other nations.

I would like to thank first and foremost Les Gelb, president, and Larry Korb, vice president and director of studies at the Council on Foreign Relations, for their support and encouragement, from the very first ideas for this project to its final words. I would also like to thank Jessica Stern, who was a senior fellow at the Council during the early days of the study group and made invaluable contributions to its organization and to the definition of the issues that the book would have to cover. Paula Dobriansky, vice president and Washington program director, and the staff of the Washington office provided key administrative and substantive support. Patricia Dorff, director of publishing at the Council, under the leadership of David Kellogg, vice president and publisher, provided superb assistance with editing and production. I have been a member of the Council for 26 years and am particularly appreciative of the strong leadership of recent years that has enhanced the Council's role in bringing informed outside input to our nation's foreign affairs.

Susan Koch, a member of the study group and deputy assistant secretary of defense, was a source of both expertise and wisdom on these subjects second to none within the U.S government. She read the manuscript and saved me from many embarrassing mistakes—all without ever getting anywhere near the necessary line between her role on this project and her government responsibilities for ongoing negotiations and policy development.

This book would simply not have been possible without the extraordinary support of Jessica Tuchman Mathews, president of the Carnegie Endowment for International Peace. Her friendship and encouragement were essential to getting through the ups and downs of writing on a policy subject whose foundations seemed to change as each chapter was drafted. She provided invaluable tangible support, including office space, the impressive Carnegie Endowment library, and access to Carnegie's magnificent team of experts on Russia, China, and proliferation. She offered important detailed comments on the manuscript and, most important, she challenged many sections where the analysis was either incomplete or just downright wrong. I cannot thank her enough.

I would also like to thank Dean Michael Rothchild and my graduate seminar at Princeton University's Woodrow Wilson School of Public and International Affairs. The semester I spent there not only forced me to organize this complex subject into a form that nonexpert readers can grasp, but gave me invaluable feedback from an extraordinary group of young scholars. Finally, my wife Elizabeth, son Eric, and daughter Kirsten never failed to offer the encouragement and help that have characterized our wonderful family for 34 years.

Jan Lodal
McLean, Virginia

Chapter 1

Clear Vision and Consistent Policies

New Threats from Weapons of Mass Destruction

Weapons of mass destruction (WMD) continue to be the most immediate serious threat to the security of the United States. While the nuclear standoff between the Soviet Union and the United States is over, nuclear, chemical, and biological weapons are increasingly the weapons of choice for states and terrorist groups who oppose the United States. Intense international cooperation will be necessary to meet this threat, especially from Russia, China, and France—permanent members of the U.N. Security Council whose veto power can block concerted multilateral action. But today, these and other nations often oppose American efforts, despite being at risk from the same threats themselves. Gaining the necessary cooperation will require major changes in U.S. policy dealing with weapons of mass destruction, starting with the elimination of vestigial Cold War nuclear missions that have no continuing value to America's security. The United States will have to choose between a growing nuclear dominance or building coalitions strong enough to control the emerging new threats.

When the Cold War came to an end under the leadership of the Soviet Union's Mikhail Gorbachev, it seemed that the threat of weapons of mass destruction could rapidly be brought under control. Russia cooperated in defeating Saddam Hussein's invasion of Kuwait, requiring Iraq to end all WMD programs, and creating the United Nations Special Commission (UNSCOM) to enforce Iraqi disarmament. Short-range nuclear weapons were dramatically reduced through the unilateral initiative taken by President George H. W. Bush to eliminate all land-based tactical and theater nuclear weapons and President Gorbachev's reciprocal action. The Nunn-Lugar Cooperative Threat Reduction program was passed by the U.S. Congress, providing financial and technical assistance to Russia in its efforts to dispose of hundreds of tons of dangerous nuclear materials, to strengthen controls on exports, and to keep weapon scientists from selling their services to the highest bidder. By 1994, Russia and the United States had worked together to persuade the three former Soviet republics of Ukraine, Kazakhstan, and Belarus to give up the nuclear weapons they inherited when the Soviet Union finally dissolved in December 1991. Thousands of weapons were moved back to Russia, averting the very real possibility that the end of the Cold War would lead to an increase in the number of nuclear weapons states. Russia and the United States undertook a cooperative effort to reduce their own nuclear forces, destroying about 25,000 nuclear weapons in the 1990s.

Arms control arrangements were also strengthened after the end of the Cold War. In January 1993, Russia and the United States signed a new Strategic Arms Reductions Treaty, START II, that requires reductions in total nuclear weapons from the 7,000-to-8,000 range permitted by START I to no more that 3,500. In 1997, agreement in principle was reached to reduce this ceiling to no more than 2,500 warheads in a future START III agreement. The Nuclear Nonproliferation Treaty (NPT), which required renewal every five years, was made permanent in 1995. The Chemical Weapons Convention (CWC) was completed in 1993 and, as was the case with the Biological Weapons Convention (BWC), almost universally accepted. If fully implemented, the CWC and BWC would eliminate all chemical and biological weapons. The United States has also strengthened its defenses against a possible chemical or biological attack on its forces and its ability to respond to a terrorist chemical or biological attack on its cities.

Notwithstanding these important and well-intended steps, the WMD challenge continues to grow. The Information Revolution is the fundamental force behind this increase.[1] It has rapidly spread the technical knowledge necessary to develop weapons of mass destruction and driven the globalization of trade and commerce that each year makes export controls harder to enforce. These changes raise the specter of rogue states, terrorists, and criminal organizations gaining access to chemical, biological, or even nuclear weapons and to the means of delivering them. They could smuggle weapons across borders, hide them in commercial vehicles or aircraft, mount them on stealthy cruise missiles, or hurl them thorough space on intercontinental ballistic missiles.

The exploding biotechnology industry has dispersed both expertise and equipment, making the development of biological weapons, both old and newer, more threatening forms, easier than ever. Tiny quantities of a biological agent can potentially kill thousands, and a few pounds properly distributed could kill millions. Chemical agents are now easy to manufacture using commercial dual-use technology available from multiple suppliers worldwide. In 1995, the Aum Shinrikyo sect in Japan was able to launch a significant chemical attack on the Tokyo subway using sarin gas that they had manufactured themselves. Although only a dozen people were killed, five thousand were injured. What is more important, terrorist groups everywhere have learned by watching the attack how to do the same thing, but much better the next time. With minor technical changes, a repeat of the Tokyo attack could kill thousands.

India and Pakistan, now declared nuclear weapons states, continue to skirmish over Kashmir, threatening a full-scale war in South Asia that could escalate to a nuclear exchange and trigger a wider war involving the major nuclear powers. At least three other states—Iraq, Iran, and North Korea—maintain active programs to develop nuclear weapons and the long-range ballistic missiles to deliver them.

Iraq's disarmament, agreed to by Saddam Hussein and required by the U.N. Security Council, was supposed to be enforced by UNSCOM. But UNSCOM has been evicted from Iraq by Saddam Hussein without completing its work. Saddam retains missiles, chemical and biological weapons, and a large technology base working on his nuclear weapons program. Iraq can now sell all the oil it can pump and as a result is earning $13 billion per year of additional hard currency. While these funds are supposed to be used only for food and medicine, this substantial increase in income permits Iraq to increase its spending on military programs. Russia, China, and France are all pressing to remove altogether the economic sanctions that remain on Iraq, leaving Saddam largely free to purchase the technologies he needs for a vigorous WMD program.[2]

The United States has made major efforts to halt Iran's efforts to develop nuclear weapons and missile technology, convincing China to provide no new assistance to Iran's nuclear program and pressing Russia to strengthen its controls on the export of sensitive technologies. But Iran continues to receive considerable outside assistance for both its nuclear and missile programs. Russia is building nuclear power plants that provide a source of nuclear expertise and possibly even bomb-making materials. North Korea provides missile technology (based on early Soviet missiles). Much dual-use technology is imported and used for WMD programs, and additional technology leaks out from Russia and other industrial nations. Iran continues to attempt to purchase nuclear materials or even a finished bomb from Russian sources.

North Korea has tested a crude version of a missile that has the capability to reach the United States. North Korea's program to develop nuclear weapons and an intercontinental ballistic missile (ICBM) to deliver them is the most dramatic of the new post–Cold War WMD threats faced by the United States. In 1994, the United

States threatened military action if North Korea refused to halt its production of plutonium for nuclear weapons. After intervention by former president Jimmy Carter, North Korea agreed to freeze its program. Diplomatic efforts led by former defense secretary William Perry have resulted in a North Korean moratorium on testing of long-range missiles. But development work on the missiles continues, and testing could be resumed on short notice. The freeze on plutonium production has remained in effect, but enough nuclear material to make one or two bombs remains unaccounted for, and the basic infrastructure needed to produce nuclear weapons is intact.

In the summer of 1999, President Bill Clinton announced that the United States would deploy a national missile defense (NMD) system based in Alaska by 2005 to meet the North Korean threat. The president made clear that the United States was moving beyond its long-standing policy favoring only research on national missile defense. But he set several conditions to be met before he would make a final deployment decision. In a speech on September 1, 2000, he announced that these conditions had not been met and that deployment would be postponed. The main reason given for the postponement was the failure of the NMD testing program to demonstrate the technical feasibility of the system: "We need more tests against more challenging targets, and more simulations before we can responsibly commit our nation's resources to deployment."[3] The president also emphasized the importance of using the time needed to perfect NMD technology to work out diplomatic differences related to NMD with U.S. allies, China, and Russia. He noted that without allied cooperation the United States would be unable to deploy some necessary components (mostly radars) overseas, and without Russian cooperation it would not be possible to maintain a modified Antiballistic Missile (ABM) Treaty. He argued that U.S. abrogation of the ABM Treaty could threaten the entire Cold War nuclear arms control regime, negotiated over a thirty-year period.

Strategic Visions

The failure of the 1999 decision to proceed with a national missile defense as the main response to the most immediate post–Cold War threat from weapons of mass destruction is symptomatic of a wider problem: the lack of a sustainable national policy for dealing with WMD. As subsequent chapters will detail, there are serious difficulties with nearly every aspect of WMD policy: nuclear strategy, antiballistic missile defenses, arms control, intelligence, and law enforcement. There is no national consensus on how to proceed. Within the U.S. Congress, there are numerous competing approaches to the problem. Even within the executive branch, there is much dissent with established policies. Many, for example, opposed the Clinton administration's decision to deploy an NMD against North Korea.

As a first step toward improving America's ability to meet the new WMD threats, the president of the United States needs to articulate a clear strategic vision that can form the basis for a comprehensive and consistent WMD policy. Today's policy is an inconsistent compromise between the three competing strategic visions most frequently espoused by members of Congress, experts and academics, administration officials, and military officers. These three visions can be summarized as follows:

STRATEGIC VISION ONE: MORE ARMS CONTROL

This vision calls for modernizing but maintaining the chief Cold War–era arms control agreements with Russia: the ABM Treaty and START. Nonproliferation is pursued by updating and enhancing the three multilateral nonproliferation conventions: the Nuclear Nonproliferation Treaty, the Chemical Weapons Convention, and the Biological Weapons Convention. U.S. ratification of the Comprehensive Test Ban Treaty helps restore American leadership in fighting nuclear proliferation. Concerns over nuclear proliferation are met largely through the stronger application of the export controls of the Wassenaar Agreement and the Missile Technology Control Regime, as well as the multilateral enforcement mechanisms of the three nonproliferation conventions. Ever-stronger bilateral and multilateral verification and enforcement institutions are developed to implement this arms control regime. No significant unilateral changes are made to the strategic and policy underpinnings of America's nuclear forces or military deployments.

STRATEGIC VISION TWO: UNDEFEATABLE ACTIVE DEFENSE

The second strategic vision has the United States focus its efforts on direct defense against weapons of mass destruction. The principal element is the deployment of a robust national antiballistic missile defense. Such a defense would be inconsistent with the 1972 ABM Treaty, which would therefore be renegotiated or unilaterally abrogated. The United States maintains or strengthens its nuclear forces in order to deter the development of WMD. It makes clear to the world that it will not tolerate threats or uses of weapons of mass destruction. Any uncertainty about the strength and reliability of America's nuclear arsenal is resolved by resuming nuclear testing. U.S. diplomats do not hesitate to threaten the use of conventional military force, or in extremis nuclear weapons, to attack preemptively and destroy threatening WMD systems because America's ABM defense provides invulnerability against long-range ballistic missiles. No attempt is made to maintain a balance of deterrence. The often-derided mutual assured destruction (MAD) doctrine is set aside;[4] reliance on nuclear deterrence eventually gives way to reliance on active defense.

STRATEGIC VISION THREE: NUCLEAR ABOLITION

The third often-espoused strategic vision focuses on the commitment included in the Nuclear Nonproliferation Treaty to abolish nuclear weapons. In May 2000 at the NPT review conference, the United States endorsed "an unequivocal undertaking by the nuclear-weapons states to accomplish the total elimination of their nuclear arsenals leading to nuclear disarmament to which all states parties are committed."[5] Thus, those supporting the strategic vision of nuclear abolition, as well as many nonnuclear foreign nations, argue that the United States has already adopted this vision as policy. Under it, the United States moves immediately (either through negotiated agreements or unilaterally if necessary) to a posture of "minimum deterrence" supported by no more than a few hundred nuclear weapons. This reduction is used to gain diplomatic leverage throughout the world for the abolition of nuclear weapons. Since the elimination of chemical and biological weapons is already called for by the CWC and the BWC, the ultimate goal is a world without any weapons of mass destruction. Multilateral enforcement mechanisms are activated to punish any state that violates the norms. Security in the United States is ensured by maintaining a posture of strong conventional forces, giving the United States the capacity to defeat any regime that violates disarmament norms.

Each of these competing visions has major weaknesses as the basis for an effective policy to control weapons of mass destruction. The first vision, more arms control, was a reasonable approach when the Cold War ended. But, as explained in Chapter 4, the arms control process has become gridlocked. Arms control as usual has lost the support of too many of the constituencies necessary for its success.

Erecting an undefeatable active defense is politically attractive but not feasible technologically. Small attacks using few warheads and no serious penetration aids can be stopped, but it is almost impossible to stop a large attack that uses many warheads, sophisticated tactics, and even simple defense-penetration aids. Furthermore, defense would also be necessary against bombers, cruise missiles, and other unconventional threats, a challenge perhaps greater than defending against ballistic missiles. Finally, long before an undefeatable defense could be constructed, other nations would move to oppose U.S. power both by building up their military capability and by forming coalitions against the United States. Arguably, the United States would be left less secure than before the buildup.

Abolition is the correct goal for chemical and biological weapons and has been accepted by almost all nations through their ratification of the Biological Weapons Convention and the Chemical Weapons Convention. But unlike chemical and biological weapons, nuclear weapons form the core of the military forces of eight nations, none of which favors abolition. Some argue that only nuclear abolition can lead to safety against WMD and that if the United States would agree to abolition, others would follow.[6] But because the United States maintains an immense nonnuclear military advantage, other powers would see a U.S. push for nuclear abolition as an effort to achieve absolute military dominance and would oppose it. Even if other countries could be persuaded to support abolition, verifying an agreement presents immense challenges. There will always be one nation that decides to keep or develop nuclear weapons secretly, since the advantage of doing so will increase as others eliminate their nuclear arsenals.

There are attractive elements in each of these three conflicting strategic visions. Current policy reflects the natural desire to keep the best of each, notwithstanding the resulting inconsistencies. START III and ABM Treaty revisions are pursued even though the Russians have refused to accept America's approach to strategic nuclear arms control. The anti–North Korea NMD is being developed to satisfy the advocates of undefeatable national defenses, even though it could be easily defeated. Nuclear forces are kept strong to provide an underlying backbone of deterrence at the same time that the commitment to eventual nuclear abolition is strengthened. What is needed is a new strategic vision that is internally consistent, protects America against the limited residual threat of nuclear war with Russia or China, and can deal with the new WMD threats stemming from terrorists and rogue states.

A NEW STRATEGIC VISION:
DETERRENCE AND COOPERATION

From the beginning of the nuclear age, it has been accepted that the primary use of nuclear weapons is to deter others from using nuclear weapons. From the beginning of modern diplomacy, it has been accepted that many national goals can be achieved only by organizing a strong coalition devoted to advancing the common interest. Controlling the spread of weapons of mass destruction will require returning to these fundamental principles and organizing a consistent policy around a strategic vision of deterrence and cooperation. The challenge will be to maintain a strong deterrence posture that does not make it impossible to obtain the widespread cooperation necessary to control the spread of weapons of mass destruction.

Deterrence is intangible, and Americans do not respond well to intangible diplomatic concepts. Deterrence is in many ways an extension of the classic balance-of-power theory that has governed Western diplomacy for three hundred years. Americans have always been suspicious of balance-of-power diplomacy, while nonetheless practicing it out of necessity. Nuclear deterrence has been an extraordinarily successful balance-of-power strategy. For fifty years it has prevented a major war, notwithstanding the intense ideological conflict between communism and the West. Arguably, America's maintenance of a strong nuclear deterrent led to the end of the Cold War. Moreover, the "tangible" alternatives to deterrence—eliminating the threat through abolition, stopping it by direct defense, or destroying it through preemptive military action—would have so many loopholes and vulnerabilities that no U.S. president would be likely to give up deterrence in favor of exclusive reliance on other mechanisms.

Even if the United States were prepared to abandon the use of nuclear deterrence, nuclear weapons would remain a major factor in world affairs. Nuclear deterrence is important in regional disputes (India and China, Pakistan and India, Israel and the Arabs) and is the only way for many states to balance America's overwhelming conventional military and economic power. The United States should explicitly acknowledge the continuing role of nuclear deterrence in its security policy and set aside the fiction that abolition or undefeatable defenses can be an adequate substitute.[7] Forthrightness would eliminate the ability of states to complain diplomatically when the United States seems not to act consistently with its professed intention of eliminating nuclear weapons. It would also help the United States regain the moral high ground in the nuclear debate.

Acknowledging the essentiality of cooperation is as important as a forthright acceptance of deterrence. The new WMD threats cannot be countered by the United States alone. They will require a concerted effort by all the world's major powers, starting with the five permanent members of the U.N. Security Council—the United States, the United Kingdom, France, Russia, and China. Today, the United States is increasingly at odds with Russia, China, and France. The reason is that these nations increasingly see the United States as a dominant, even hegemonic, power that must be resisted if their nations' economic independence, cultural heritage, and political systems are to survive. The challenge facing any hegemonic power is to achieve acceptance of its policies. If the United States frequently uses its dominant force to work its will, coalitions will develop against it, including even "friendly" nations. Such a process is already apparent. The United States will have to compromise to avoid further movements in this direction, more and more of which will involve the development of nuclear and other weapons of mass destruction as the only practical means of balancing American military power.

If America's dominance were only in "soft power"—financial, political, and cultural—perhaps there would be no opposition to American efforts to stop the proliferation of WMD. But America's military dominance is even more complete than its soft power dominance. At the heart of this dominance is America's overwhelming offensive nuclear force. If the United States were to add a significant active defense against nuclear attack to its dominant offensive force, starting with a national missile defense, America could develop a true "first-strike" capability— the capability to launch a preemptive attack against another power and retain enough offensive and defensive forces to deter retaliation. This would be the ultimate military capability— enough force to threaten the survival of any rival. Of course, launching a preemptive attack for any reason short of stopping an inevitable WMD attack against the United States would be contrary to all American traditions and values. But just as the United States has always insisted on evaluating any potential adversary's capabilities rather than its intentions, other nations will evaluate U.S. capabilities in making their own decisions about how to respond to the United States.

The United States and Russia agreed at Helsinki in 1997 that a START III treaty would include a ceiling on strategic nuclear weapons of 2,500. This ceiling would not cover shorter-range nuclear weapons launchable from aircraft or submarines, of which probably 1,000 or more would be retained. A level of 3,500 active nuclear weapons would represent a reduction of more than 85 percent from the height of the Cold War. But 3,500 weapons would still be quantitatively more than double what Russia plans to maintain and more than 100 times the size of China's force. Qualitatively, the American force would be vastly superior—more reliable and much more flexible and survivable. When combined with an NMD capable of intercepting several hundred incoming warheads, it would constitute a true first-strike force, even at the much reduced START III levels.

The United States has refused to consider strategic nuclear forces smaller than 2,500 weapons because the U.S. military says that 2,500 are needed to implement America's nuclear war planning guidance. As explained in Chapter 2, the war planning guidance that stands in the way of smaller forces is the requirement to plan for a "prompt retaliatory" attack to support the mission of limiting damage should nuclear war break out. The prompt retaliatory war plan requires being able to launch an all-out attack against Russian strategic forces with little warning. This is identical to what is required of a preemptive attack, so the prompt retaliatory option constitutes de facto a preemptive attack plan. However the United States characterizes this plan, it can only be seen by the Russians as a major component of a complete first-strike capability.[8]

There is no continuing reason to retain the guidance that requires a prompt retaliatory war plan. U.S. nuclear strategy should be limited to deterring nuclear attack, balancing Russian nuclear power, and a very few other limited nuclear missions. With a new strategy, the role and number of nuclear weapons could be reduced significantly from today's levels. There is also a role for antiballistic missile defenses within a strategic vision of deterrence and cooperation but for limited defenses of a much different character than the NMD currently being pursued. A decision by the United States to reduce its offensive forces below 2,500 and to adopt a nonthreatening approach to strategic defenses would be a powerful answer to those who believe the United States is committed to hegemonic military dominance.

Arms control can continue to play an important part in implementing a strategic vision of deterrence and cooperation. But arms control itself cannot be the objective of U.S. policy, and agreements must be adaptable over time to avoid losing their effectiveness. To this end, a new agreement, which could be titled the Strategic Transparency, Safety, and Stability treaty (STRANSS), should replace the ABM and START treaties as the focus of future nuclear arms control agreements with Russia. STRANSS should incorporate and strengthen those provisions of the ABM Treaty committing Russia and the United States to avoid developing first-strike capabilities against each other. But it should move away from the detailed numeric controls that are no longer an important measure of military capability, are not necessary for verification, and have become an impediment to the rational restructuring of nuclear forces in both nations.

The chapters that follow set forth a detailed, integrated approach to implementing a new national policy dealing with weapons of mass destruction. The approach begins with abandoning remaining Cold War theory and practice that no longer apply to the new threats the United States faces today. The prompt retaliatory nuclear war plan must be dropped in favor of a nuclear strategy and force structure focused on deterrence. The Cold War ABM and START treaties should be replaced by STRANSS, a more appropriate bilateral agreement with Russia. The United States must settle the nuclear confrontation left over from the Cold War on terms that convince Russia, China, and France that the United States does not seek absolute military dominance, if it is to obtain the cooperation needed to control the new WMD threats.

Other changes must also be made. The focus of nuclear strategy needs to shift from Europe to Asia. Reliance on multilateral agencies to enforce chemical, biological, and nuclear nonproliferation should give way to a combination of cooperative alliances and the traditional enforcement methods of diplomacy, sanctions, isolation, and military force. The crucial roles of law enforcement and intelligence must be dramatically strengthened, especially through much greater international cooperation. Finally, the United States must use its new policies based on deterrence and cooperation to reinvigorate its leadership in the struggle to contain the growing threat of WMD.

The specific steps necessary to carry out a shift to a policy based on deterrence and cooperation are summarized in the following lists and elaborated in subsequent chapters.

A Consistent New Policy Summarized

NUCLEAR STRATEGY

1. Balance Russian forces by maintaining deterrence through second-strike retaliation. Deterrence must be strong enough both to deter a direct nuclear attack and to eliminate a Russian threat of nuclear attack as diplomatic leverage in a crisis.

2. Maintain a "nuclear umbrella" over Japan and South Korea (and implicitly Southeast Asia) while China modernizes and expands its nuclear force. Maintain a de facto nuclear umbrella over Europe but do so focused on reassuring Germany that it need not consider developing its own nuclear weapons.

3. Drop the damage-limiting mission for using nuclear forces against Russia and the associated prompt retaliatory war plans that appear to Russia, China, and others as first-strike war plans.

4. Assign only four limited first-use missions to U.S. nuclear forces:

   • Retaliate against a nonnuclear WMD attack on the United States, its forces, or its allies when conventional retaliation cannot bring the WMD attacks to an immediate halt.

   • Preempt a nonnuclear WMD attack when intelligence indicates that such an attack is imminent and conventional preemption is not feasible.

   • Hold at risk deep underground WMD facilities that cannot be dealt with by other military means and would otherwise permit a hostile rogue state or a terrorist organization to develop weapons of mass destruction.

   • Hold at risk the ability of nuclear powers other than Russia to carry out nuclear attacks against the United States and its allies if a major conventional war were to break out, a nuclear attack seemed imminent, and preemption with conventional forces was not feasible.

5. Provide continuing monetary and technical assistance to Russia for restructuring, dismantling, and ensuring the safety and security of its nuclear forces.

NUCLEAR FORCES

1. Adjust to the elimination of prompt retaliatory war plans by reducing U.S. strategic nuclear forces to 1,000 highly survivable weapons: 160 weapons on B-2 bombers and 840 on submarine-launched ballistic missiles (SLBMs). Retain all 14 Trident nuclear submarines (SSBNs), and rotate SLBMs off submarines when they return to port, keeping all missiles alert at sea and therefore invulnerable to attack.

2. Reduce nonstrategic nuclear weapons in Europe from about 500 to 200 and eliminate the roughly 500 intermediate-range nuclear cruise missiles (submarine- and air-launched) now kept in reserve.

BALLISTIC MISSILE DEFENSES

1. Assign five strategic missions to ballistic missile defenses:

    -   Protect U.S. troops in the field against theater ballistic missiles.

    -   Defend the United States should deterrence of rogue states such as North Korea, Iran, or Iraq fail.

    -   Provide insurance against the unlikely occurrence of an accidental launch.

    -   In times of crisis, defend the cities of U.S. friends and allies against WMD-capable ballistic missiles.

    -   Enhance deterrence in a crisis by making it necessary for an adversary to launch a relatively large nuclear attack against the U.S. homeland (more than 25 to 50 warheads) to overcome the defense.

2. Focus ballistic missile defense (BMD) programs on deploying theater missile defense (TMD) systems, mobile "boost-phase" systems capable of serving multiple strategic missions, and a land-based national missile defense with 100 ground-based interceptors deployed at multiple sites.

3. Leverage unilateral changes in U.S. nuclear strategy and deployments to obtain an international consensus supporting a new balance between offense and defense.

4. Offer to share space-based ballistic missile warning and tracking systems widely and to provide mobile TMD protection to friends and allies in times of crisis.

5. Anticipate increases in China's deployments of nuclear ballistic missiles.

NUCLEAR ARMS CONTROL

1. In place of the START III and ABM treaties, negotiate a new Strategic Transparency, Safety, and Stability treaty with

Russia. STRANSS should preserve the no-first-strike principles of the Cold War nuclear treaty regime while providing the flexibility necessary to carry out the five strategic missions assigned above to ballistic missile defenses.

2. Focus on preventing new threats by increasing the priority of nuclear nonproliferation in U.S. diplomacy and being better prepared to organize sanctions, isolation, or military force to stop proliferation by rogue states or terrorists.[9]

3. Make the Nuclear Nonproliferation Treaty the centerpiece of nonproliferation arms control, supported by other institutions such as the Missile Technology Control Regime, the Zangger Committee, and the Fissile Material Cutoff Treaty. Work to bring India, Pakistan, and Israel into compliance with NPT norms. Defer resubmitting the Comprehensive Test Ban Treaty to the Senate until India agrees to sign it.

ENFORCING CHEMICAL AND BIOLOGICAL WEAPONS ABOLITION

1. Rely on U.S. and other nations' intelligence services to detect noncompliance with the chemical and biological weapons conventions.

2. Use the United Nations and other multilateral organizations to audit reports prepared by all states detailing any chemical and biological weapons-related activities, including each state's domestic law enforcement efforts focused on enforcing the CWC and the BWC.

3. Enhance deterrence of terrorist or rogue-state attacks on U.S. citizens and troops by further strengthening passive defenses and emergency response capabilities.

4. Work to achieve an international consensus on strong diplomatic, economic, and military actions to be taken against states that refuse to accept or do not comply with the CWC and the BWC.

INTELLIGENCE AND LAW ENFORCEMENT

1. Acknowledge that communications intelligence will become increasingly difficult as encryption technology continues to spread. Nevertheless, complicate terrorists' operations by requiring businesses to escrow encryption keys used for commercial transactions.

2. Offset the diminishing effectiveness of technical intelligence by increasing resources devoted to human intelligence (HUMINT), primarily through greatly increased international cooperation.

3. Develop a secure intermediary to receive raw intelligence related to prohibited WMD activities, protect sources and methods, integrate and fuse finished intelligence products, and share them with international organizations and other states. Consider using a small, trusted state such as New Zealand, Switzerland, or Sweden to serve this function.

4. Assign a law enforcement cooperation officer to each ambassador's country team with broad authority over the efforts of all U.S. law enforcement organizations inside that country.

5. Increase even further the budgets of U.S. law enforcement agencies devoted to countering WMD terrorism and proliferation.

LEADERSHIP AND CONSISTENCY

1. Accept that the challenge posed by the proliferation of weapons of mass destruction cannot be met without both American leadership and international cooperation.

2. Restore consistency in American policy by moving to an unambiguously defensive nuclear posture, emphasizing the continuing importance of nuclear deterrence while reducing nuclear offensive forces to 1,200 survivable warheads.

3. Acknowledge the necessity of developing coalitions to control the threat of WMD, with special effort placed on achieving open cooperation with China, France, India, Pakistan, and Russia.

4. Continue to support arms control as an important element of international cooperation but restructure the bilateral Cold War treaties with Russia to focus on strategic transparency, safety, and stability and revise the role of multilateral enforcement organizations.

5. Increase the U.S. government's budget by $5 billion a year for intelligence, diplomatic operations, and foreign assistance to support efforts against weapons of mass destruction.

These changes constitute a large agenda. It is tempting to choose among them. Variations and adjustments in the details are always possible. But America can capitalize on its unique position in history only with a clear strategic vision implemented in a consistent manner. Doing so will require much more than marginal adjustments to long-standing policies; all of the issues dealt with by the far-reaching changes outlined above must be addressed to create a new regime based on deterrence and cooperation.

Notes

1. Jessica T. Mathews, "The Information Revolution," *Foreign Policy* 119 (Summer 2000), pp. 63–65.

2. Richard Butler, *The Greatest Threat* (New York: Public Affairs, 2000).

3. William J. Clinton, "Remarks by the President on National Missile Defense," September 1, 2000, www.pub.whitehouse.gov/uri-res/12R?urn://oma.eop.gov.us/2000/9/1/9.text.1.

4. The term "mutual assured destruction" was coined by opponents of deterrence and never used officially to describe U.S. policy.

5. The word "unequivocal" was used for the first time after pressure from states unhappy with earlier use by the nuclear powers of qualifiers such as "eventual."

6. Jonathan Schell, "The Folly of Arms Control," *Foreign Affairs* 75, no. 5 (September/October 2000), pp. 22–46.

7. Unfortunately, U.S. statements at the 2000 NPT Review Conference added to this confusion. The only alternative, short of renouncing the NPT, which would be a mistake, is to return to the position that the commitment to abolition has no target date and is only an ultimate goal to which we cannot see a path today.

8. "Prompt retaliatory" connotes the ability to retaliate as soon as it is clear that war has begun—perhaps even before any nuclear weapons have detonated on U.S. targets. Maintaining the ability to execute such a plan requires a high level of alert, since warning times could be as short as a few minutes.

9. Ashton B. Carter and William J. Perry, *Preventive Defense* (Washington, D.C.: Brookings Institution Press, 1999).

Chapter 2

Nuclear Strategy and Forces

Cold War Nuclear Missions

DETERRENCE AND ASSURED RETALIATION

In August 1945, the world was changed forever when two crude atomic bombs were dropped on Hiroshima and Nagasaki. One hundred fifty thousand people were killed instantly and another 70,000 eventually died.[1] By 1961, the United States had a stockpile of nuclear weapons that numbered 24,173, and the Soviet Union had 2,471 nuclear weapons. By 1988, the United States and the Soviet Union together possessed 65,000 nuclear weapons, an inconceivable amount of destructive power.[2] A superpower nuclear war would have inevitably expanded to Western Europe, China, and Japan, killing perhaps half of all humanity.

Such a nuclear holocaust was averted by the painstaking creation of a regime of nuclear deterrence. Rather than use nuclear weapons as offensive weapons of war, it has been the bedrock principle of nuclear strategy since the earliest days of the nuclear age to maintain them to deter an adversary's use of its nuclear weapons. Maintaining the capability to absorb a nuclear attack, retaliate, and cause unacceptable damage to the attacker is central to deterring a nuclear attack. Ensuring this capability has been the focus of U.S. nuclear weapons programs since the Soviet Union developed the capability to threaten the U.S. homeland directly.

The ability to retaliate is basic, but ensuring that there are no weaknesses in the complex fabric of deterrence requires attention to many other details. By the mid-1950s, the Soviet Union had developed the capacity to target American nuclear forces, creating concerns about "crisis stability." Crisis stability requires that one's nuclear weapon systems not present an attractive target for a preemptive strike. An enemy might be able to destroy much of an adversary's retaliatory capability with a preemptive strike while retaining enough force to deter the adversary's retaliation with its now-debilitated retaliatory force. If so, a nuclear war might actually be motivated by a nation's nuclear force rather than deterred by it. Thus, invulnerable submarines, hardened intercontinental ballistic missiles, and alert bombers able to take off on warning of attack have composed the U.S. strategic nuclear force. The United States has never promised to "ride out" a nuclear attack on its forces, but it has always attempted to maintain its capacity to do so.

FIRST-USE MISSIONS

Although deterrence theory has dominated U.S. nuclear strategy and policy, traditional military considerations have dominated preparations for nuclear war. The two nuclear bombs used against Japan brought World War II to an end. This was a traditional war-fighting use of a new and better weapon. Years before Russia developed a credible capability to threaten the United States, the U.S. Air Force planned and trained to use the massive firepower of nuclear weapons to defeat the Soviet Union in a war in Europe. These plans became the basis of the Eisenhower administration's strategy of "massive retaliation." Massive retaliation called for nuclear retaliation not only against a Soviet nuclear attack but also against a ground force invasion of Western Europe.

Starting in the late 1950s, the United States began the deployment of thousands of tactical nuclear weapons to permit a "flexible response" to a Soviet invasion of Europe or a Chinese invasion of Korea. Flexible response required that a range of options be available to respond, from conventional weapons through tactical nuclear weapons up to strategic nuclear weapons. More than 12,000 tactical nuclear weapons were eventually built to support this strategy. Most were in Europe, but substantial numbers were also deployed in South Korea and even Japan, notwithstanding Japan's post-Hiroshima nuclear aversion.

Tactical nuclear weapons have attracted less public attention than have strategic intercontinental weapons. Yet these weapons have always been the ones most likely to be used first in a nuclear war. A nuclear war would almost certainly begin as an escalation from a conventional war between nuclear powers. One side or the other would eventually begin to lose the war, at which point it would seriously consider using tactical nuclear weapons to reverse the tide of battle. In contrast, using strategic nuclear weapons to start a war with a "bolt out of the blue" has always been an unlikely scenario.

Many of the 12,000 U.S. and 20,000 Soviet tactical nuclear weapons were more powerful than the Hiroshima and Nagasaki bombs. A tactical nuclear war would have killed tens or perhaps hundreds of millions, even without escalating to an all-out strategic nuclear exchange. But such a war probably would have escalated. Tactical nuclear weapons would not have led to a decisive outcome on the battlefield, but their use would have broken the taboo against nuclear weapons. At some point, one side would begin to lose the tactical nuclear war. With a large strategic nuclear force in reserve, the losing side would have a strong incentive to escalate the war and use strategic forces in an attempt to regain the military initiative.

NATO's European members accepted this scenario, with its catastrophic outcome, as the best possible deterrent of a Soviet invasion. If the Soviets knew that the outcome would be catastrophic, the theory went, they would never start a conventional war. Of course, if it did start, either NATO's bluff would be called, or the war would lead to the destruction of Europe. These were not good choices, which is why the United States put so much pressure on Europe to improve its conventional forces and reduce reliance on tactical nuclear weapons.

Some wondered whether NATO might not have been too clever with this strategy, leading the Soviets to conclude that NATO was, in fact, bluffing. If the Soviets thought NATO would never escalate to nuclear weapons, they might try to conquer all of Europe. To undercut such skepticism, elaborate plans were drawn up for the use of tactical nuclear weapons, and troops were carefully trained. The command-and-control system that released authority to respond with nuclear weapons was frequently tested and authorized. Planners estimated the size and dispersion of potential enemy invasion forces and calculated the quantity of tactical nuclear weapons necessary to destroy those forces, keeping in reserve enough weapons to deter a counterattack on allied cities. Plans had to account for weapon reliability (15 to 30 percent of the weapons were assumed to fail) and the battlefield destruction of some weapons. When all these factors were considered, thousands of weapons were judged necessary to destroy the dispersed Soviet conventional military force the United States and its NATO allies faced at the height of the Cold War, notwithstanding the enormous explosive power of each nuclear weapon. Thus, thousands of nuclear weapons were deployed, which itself became the best evidence of NATO's intent to use nuclear weapons first if necessary, no matter how high the risk of a catastrophic outcome.

America's threat to use nuclear weapons first has been a key element in providing extended deterrence. Plans for using nuclear weapons against nonnuclear threats have involved responding to threats against allies or against American forces deployed to defend allies. Using America's nuclear power to deal with the threats posed by China and Russia to its allies has been labeled "extended deterrence." The word "extended" usually refers to extending the deterrent capability of American nuclear forces to protect other nations against nuclear attack, but it also refers to extending the deterrence mission of nuclear weapons from that of deterring nuclear attacks to deterring nonnuclear attacks when conventional forces are inadequate to do so.

Plans to use nuclear weapons to preempt or retaliate against non-nuclear attacks have not been limited to stopping a massive invasion of Western Europe or South Korea. Today the focus of such plans is on deterring the use of chemical or biological weapons. This is a relatively noncontroversial mission for nuclear weapons, but it does present diplomatic difficulties. In 1968, in conjunction with signing the NPT, the United States pledged not to use nuclear weapons first against a power that was a member in good standing of the NPT, had no nuclear weapons, and was not allied with a nuclear power.[3] However, as the threat of chemical and biological attack has grown, the position of the United States has changed. It has taken pains not to rule out any response to a WMD attack, including a nuclear response. The threat of using nuclear weapons first in a confrontation with a power possessing WMD thus remains very much a part of U.S. overall nuclear policy. There is evidence that this strategy has worked: During the 1991 Persian Gulf war, the threat of nuclear retaliation was used to deter Saddam Hussein's use of chemical or biological warheads on Scud missiles.

The largest planned first-use nuclear attacks are "counterforce" attacks—attacks designed to limit damage to the United States should deterrence fail and nuclear war occur. The idea of damage limitation is to attack and destroy enemy forces before they can be used. This mission has absorbed the greatest number of strategic nuclear weapons in America's nuclear war plan, the Single Integrated Operations Plan (SIOP). Since many enemy nuclear forces are dispersed or hardened, to destroy them with any degree of certainty requires that multiple nuclear weapons be used against each target. If there is any chance that a target might contain an unused weapon or accommodate a "reload," the war planners will target multiple warheads against it. The result is to generate a "requirement" for thousands of weapons to be used against missile silos, bomber bases, and command structures, many of which will probably be empty if the attack is retaliatory. Destroying empty missile silos or bomber bases after their weapons have been launched is planned nevertheless, both because it is uncertain which are empty and to prevent reloads.

The SIOP's main damage-limiting attack is designed as a "prompt retaliatory" attack, not as an attack that would be undertaken hours or days after a nuclear war began. Prompt retaliation is considered important to destroy as many enemy weapons as possible before they can be used and to use as many American weapons as possible before they are destroyed on the ground. As a result, such an attack would have to be launched either in the fifteen to twenty minutes available after an incoming attack was unambiguously detected ("launch under attack") or launched preemptively. Although launch under attack is a theoretical possibility, it is not a practical reality. The command-and-control challenges involved in having the president decide to undertake such an action are difficult. American forces are designed to withstand a surprise attack precisely to avoid the necessity of hasty decisions. In practice, then, if the prompt retaliatory attack option were used at all, it would be used preemptively.

Throughout the Cold War, the focus of U.S. policy was to prevent a nuclear war with Russia. The irony is that implementing America's threat to be the one that starts the nuclear war—to be the first to use nuclear weapons, either to stop a conventional attack by Russia or China or to limit damage once war seemed inevitable—was the greatest focus of U.S. nuclear war plans. Fortunately, the strength of deterrence prevailed, and the Cold War ended without a Soviet or Chinese nuclear attack and, with one exception, without a crisis that might have led to America's first use of nuclear weapons.[4]

Post–Cold War Nuclear Missions

BALANCING RUSSIAN NUCLEAR FORCES

Russia still maintains more than 5,000 active strategic nuclear weapons and plans to maintain at least 1,500, even if its preferred arms control outcome is achieved. Perhaps another 20,000 weapons remain inactive in storage, waiting to be dismantled and destroyed.

While the end of the Cold War has meant the end of hostility between Russia and the United States, with a Russian force of this size it would be highly imprudent to rely on political good-will alone as protection against the possibility of nuclear attack. Deterring a Russian attack should remain the primary mission of U.S. nuclear forces. Further, without a strong nuclear deterrent, Russia might attempt to use its nuclear power as leverage to achieve diplomatic objectives, especially in a crisis. Some of President Vladimir Putin's statements on nuclear weapons imply that this is Russia's plan.

EXTENDED DETERRENCE IN ASIA

Deterrence of nuclear attack also continues to be important in Asia. The United States has a treaty commitment to defend Japan. The U.S. nuclear umbrella is a major part of that security commitment. It gives Japan considerable assurance that its long-term security needs can be met without Japan becoming a nuclear power. Japan is profoundly schizophrenic about the proper role of nuclear weapons. Being the only nation to have experienced a nuclear attack, Japan has a strong anti-nuclear movement, made even stronger by its large antiwar pacifist movement. At the same time, if Japan were left alone to defend itself in Asia, nationalistic pressures would almost certainly force the development of an independent Japanese nuclear deterrent. China has a substantial nuclear force, and North Korea may already have one or two nuclear weapons. South Korea certainly has the capability to develop nuclear weapons. A unified Korea could pose a second nuclear threat to Japan. Given the short flight times of ballistic missiles from Korea or China, Japan would almost certainly insist on both an active ballistic missile defense of its islands and an independent nuclear deterrent if the United States were to withdraw its nuclear umbrella.

The United States also maintains an implicit nuclear umbrella over Taiwan. The Taiwan Relations Act requires the United States to ensure the military security of Taiwan: "It is the policy of the United States . . . to provide Taiwan with arms of defensive character; and to maintain the capacity of the United States to resist any resort to force or other forms of coercion that would jeopardize the security, or the social or economic system, of the people on Taiwan."[5] Taiwan has the ability to develop an independent nuclear force but has refrained from doing so under U.S. pressure. Taiwan will almost certainly continue to accept the implicit and somewhat weak U.S. nuclear umbrella as an alternative to its own nuclear force. It knows that developing a nuclear force of its own would provoke a confrontation with China, which Taiwan would ultimately lose. If the United States were to withdraw its nuclear guarantee explicitly, however, Taiwan might well feel compelled to risk developing at least a covert nuclear capability, such as Israel has.

After years of support from the United States, the South Korean military is now capable of defending its homeland against a conventional invasion from North Korea. South Korea would need air power and other support from the United States, but it would not need nuclear weapons. It was never clear that nuclear weapons would provide a decisive advantage in any case. There are no longer any ground-launched tactical nuclear weapons in the U.S. arsenal and no plans to use the few remaining theater and strategic weapons in a conventional war in Asia.

DROPPING EXTENDED DETERRENCE IN EUROPE AND DAMAGE LIMITING

With the end of the Cold War, Russia has lost its capability to invade Western Europe with conventional forces. These forces are in shambles, unable to deal with the Chechnya challenge, and there are no longer Warsaw Pact allies to absorb initial NATO attacks or to provide a substantial portion of an attack force. Even if the Russians were to mount a massive effort to rebuild a conventional threat to Europe, which is an almost inconceivable political step, it would take them decades to do so. Moreover, the United States and its NATO allies can certainly enhance their conventional forces enough to defend themselves effectively before a threat emerges.

President George Bush realized this when he unilaterally deactivated and began to dismantle all U.S. tactical nuclear weapons in September 1991.[6] Only a few hundred aircraft-delivered nuclear bombs remain in Europe to support flexible response, along with a comparable number of British and French warheads. Nevertheless, flexible response remains the official policy of NATO, the United States, Britain, and France. Nuclear forces are still maintained with a mission to repel a land invasion of Europe. But the threat that once justified nuclear forces designed to strike first against the Russian army is simply no longer present.

The other first-use mission against Russia is the damage-limiting mission. Russia continues to maintain a large nuclear force, and, in principle, the damage-limitation mission remains valid. Yet, since the mid-1960s the reality was that Soviet (now Russian) forces were so large and well protected that effective damage limitation was impossible. An all-out war would essentially destroy all major U.S. cities and military facilities, no matter how many offensive weapons were devoted to the damage-limitation task. If START II is implemented, Russia will phase out its land-based ICBMs equipped with multiple independently targetable reentry vehicles (MIRVs), the most attractive damage-limiting targets—up to ten warheads could be eliminated by destroying a single fixed ICBM silo. This change will make damage limiting even more problematic.[7]

The first-use missions of extended deterrence and damage limitation have done more to determine U.S. nuclear policy and force structure than has the mission of deterring attack by maintaining an assured second-strike capability. Most of the U.S. nuclear force structure has been dedicated to these first-use missions in SIOP and theater nuclear war plans; only a few hundred survivable second-strike weapons have been thought necessary to deter a sudden nuclear attack on the United States. Yet the political rhetoric associated with nuclear weapons has implied a need for large numbers of weapons to deter a Soviet or Chinese surprise nuclear attack. Part of this contradiction can be explained by the emergence of a deterrence doctrine that was independent of actual war plans or the destructive capacity of the nuclear force:

the doctrine of "essential equivalence." According to this theory (discussed in the context of its impact on arms control in Chapter 4), parity in nuclear firepower is necessary for deterrence. With the acceptance of the essential equivalence doctrine, weapons were maintained that were not needed for second-strike retaliation, so war plans allocated many of them to the first-use missions of extended deterrence in Europe and damage limiting. Since these missions no longer have any rationale, there is no longer any justification for maintaining war plans or forces to support them.

A "NO-FIRST-USE" PLEDGE?

With these changes, the United States would be close to adopting a no-first-use pledge. As mentioned above, the United States has offered a limited no-first-use pledge in conjunction with the NPT. Additional no-first-use pledges have been incorporated into various nuclear-free-zone agreements. President Bush's elimination of tactical nuclear weapons meant that the primary first-use instrument was no longer available to the American military, furthering the move away from dependence on the first use of nuclear weapons. Removing prompt retaliatory attack options from war plans and announcing that no such plans will be maintained as a matter of policy would be another step toward a no-first-use policy.

But taking the final step of making an explicit no-first-use pledge would be a mistake. Four limited but valid first-use missions remain for nuclear forces:

- To destroy deep underground WMD facilities, several of which have been constructed by rogue states. Should such a facility contain weapons of mass destruction, it might be in the interest of the United States to destroy the facility preemptively. Only nuclear weapons are capable of destroying many deep underground facilities.[8]

- To preempt a WMD attack by a rogue state or terrorist group. If intelligence indicates an imminent WMD attack, conventional forces may be too slow or too overt to preempt the attack.

- To retaliate against a nonnuclear WMD attack on the United States, its forces, or its allies when conventional retaliation cannot bring the WMD attacks to an immediate halt.

- If a major war were to break out, a nuclear attack seemed imminent, and the destruction of enemy nuclear forces with conventional forces was not feasible, to preempt the ability of nuclear powers other than Russia or China to launch nuclear attacks against the United States or its allies.

These missions are purely military, in the sense that they could be accomplished by conventional military forces if the technology were available. Even today, no American president would authorize the use of nuclear weapons in even these extreme circumstances until all nonnuclear military options had been exhausted. But until conventional forces are capable of carrying out these missions, it would be wrong to deny that the possibility of using nuclear weapons to accomplish them confers a significant military advantage. If the United States gave up these nuclear missions, it would be largely in response to antinuclear diplomatic and political pressures. Many of those pushing for a no-first-use pledge will not be satisfied with anything short of the abolition of all nuclear weapons in any event, and abolition is not a realistic alternative in the foreseeable future. Even if all first-use missions were renounced, an existential first-use capability would remain. Notwithstanding a no-first-use pledge, an American president might respond with nuclear weapons to a nonnuclear WMD attack. But a pledge could motivate a hostile and irrational government to conclude that war threatening U.S. vital interests could be fought without risk of a U.S. nuclear response. An unconditional no-first-use pledge by the United States might contribute to just such a tragic misjudgment.

A Nuclear Force for the 21st Century

In 1997, the Clinton administration conducted a review of nuclear deployments. That review concluded, with support from the Joint

Chiefs of Staff, that strategic nuclear weapons could be reduced from 3,500 to 2,500 if Russia did likewise. The result was the agreement reached between President Boris Yeltsin and President Clinton at Helsinki in March 1997 calling for START III to reduce warheads to a final level of 2,000 to 2,500. The logic for this change was a conclusion that a Russian reduction to 2,500 deployed weapons would also reduce the number of targets that U.S. forces would have to attack in a prompt retaliatory damage-limiting strike. These numbers were considered adequate to carry out the existing nuclear war planning guidance that had been provided to the United States Strategic Command after the 1994 Nuclear Posture Review.

Some have argued that the present U.S. criteria for planning nuclear strikes cannot be further adjusted to permit reductions below 2,500 because that is the minimum number necessary to develop war plans consistent with present policy (and even then only if the Russians reduce to no more than 2,500). But the weakness of this argument is that the scenario driving the number of weapons needed for nuclear war plans—a preemptive or prompt retaliatory damage-limiting strike against Russia—no longer makes sense.

Even if one sees the need to hedge against a possibly resurgent Russia under a radically different, nondemocratic government attempting to use its nuclear weapons as leverage, it is impossible to foresee circumstances in which the United States would choose to start an all-out nuclear war. Throughout the Cold War, the most likely nuclear war scenario was NATO's first use of tactical nuclear weapons to stop a Soviet invasion of Western Europe. Had a tactical nuclear war in Europe broken out, both the rationale and the pressure for a damage-limiting preemptive strike against Soviet strategic nuclear forces would have been strong. Even so, the amount of damage limiting possible would have been small relative to the almost inevitable catastrophe of the all-out nuclear exchange that would have ensued. Today, there is simply no scenario in which an American president would launch a preemptive or prompt retaliatory attack.

If the prompt retaliatory option and its associated first-strike capabilities against Russia were eliminated from U.S. strategic war plans, the remaining mission of deterrence through assured retaliation could be carried out with fewer than 1,000 survivable weapons. The planned START III force structure of 2,500 weapons total incorporates only about 1,000 "survivable" weapons. Significant portions of American weapons are vulnerable to destruction in a Russian attack. Essentially all weapons, the SLBM force in port for rotation, training, and repair (normally about half the force), and all B-2 bombers at their bases could be destroyed in a surprise attack. As a result, with the proposed force of 2,500 weapons there would be only about 500 weapons surviving that could be used in a second-strike retaliatory attack plan (assuming a small reserve and allowing for unreliable systems). Even a "generated" retaliatory attack (retaliation after having received strategic warning and placing all possible weapons on alert) would have available only about 1,000 weapons. Retaliatory attacks of either size would destroy Russia's economy, major cities, and leadership. Since military and civilian defense planners have pronounced 2,500 total weapons adequate to deter a Russian attack, they have implicitly agreed that a surviving retaliatory force of 500 to 1,000 is adequate. This is about the capability of the 400 "equivalent megatons" accepted as the standard for the "assured destruction" of the Soviet Union since Secretary of Defense Robert McNamara first specified the assured destruction retaliatory mission as the primary component of nuclear deterrence in the mid-1960s.

The United States can restructure its forces so that a total force of 1,000 weapons is nearly completely survivable. Most could be deployed at sea, where they are essentially completely invulnerable. A few weapons should be deployed on B-2 aircraft to provide a flexible response nuclear force that can be used in extremis to destroy targets not easily covered by submarine-launched missiles and to carry out the very limited military missions listed above. A reasonable split of forces would be 840 warheads on SLBMs and 160 carried on 20 B-2s.

To be 100 percent survivable, all 840 sea-based weapons should be kept permanently at sea. This can be achieved by transferring missiles from submarines as they return to port for necessary rotations.[9] The present force of 14 active submarines could then accommodate 840 at sea, loading 5 warheads on each of the 24 D-5 missiles carried on each at-sea boat (the missiles can carry up to 8 warheads). The result would be 7 boats at sea (following current rotation policies of being in port 50 percent of the time) equipped with 120 warheads each, for a total of 840 invulnerable warheads at sea. In times of crisis, the missiles could be distributed among more than 7 submarines at sea, increasing both force survivability and targeting flexibility.

These changes in operating procedures would be costly but much less expensive than maintaining the much larger 2,500-warhead force anticipated under current force plans. The changes would also require modifications in the verification rules used in START agreements to date. As indicated in Chapter 4, however, the START model has largely run its course. The next round of offensive arms control agreements should permit the type of flexibility outlined. It is in the interest of both the United States and Russia to do so, since the first-strike threat against missiles on submarines in port would be eliminated. This vulnerability has always been a potential source of strategic instability since missile-loaded in-port submarines present such a valuable preemption target.

A strategic nuclear force of B-2 bombers and Trident SSBNs would mean the end of the "triad" of land-based, sea-based, and bomber-based strategic forces. The triad ensured the reliability and survivability of America's strategic retaliatory force for 40 years. By presenting multiple target types, the triad made destroying the force in a preemptive attack difficult. The multiple systems also meant that an unexpected catastrophic failure in any one system still left a large retaliatory force. Land-based ICBMs have played a particularly important role, and many will argue that they must be retained. The command-and-control system that links them to the national command authority is more flexible and reliable than is the system for communicating with deployed nuclear missile submarines. ICBMs were at one time more accurate than SLBMs. Today, these advantages are waning. Technology has improved SLBM accuracy to essentially that of ICBMs. In any event, if the damage-limiting mission is set aside, as recommended, there is no need for a large number of highly accurate weapons. The command-and-control advantages of ICBMs were most apparent in planning for prompt responses or in nuclear-war-fighting scenarios, which are also irrelevant if the only mission in the SIOP is deterrence through retaliation.

The proposed force would also have all the command-and-control and targeting flexibility needed to carry out the limited first-use missions identified above. Additional capabilities, however, should be added to the B-2 force by configuring more weapon types to fit on aircraft. The deep-penetrating nuclear weapon in development could hold deep underground targets more at risk and should be added to the active force. Low-yield weapons should be available to provide more attack flexibility, and a few nuclear air-launched cruise missiles should be converted from B-52s to B-2s to allow limited single-weapon standoff attacks. A dozen weapons in each category would be adequate.[10]

The United States also maintains the capacity to deploy up to 500 nuclear bombs in Europe to carry out NATO's flexible response strategy. As explained above, this strategy no longer has any meaning since Russia has no capability to mount the attack that flexible response is meant to deter. These weapons could thus be eliminated entirely if flexible response were the only reason for keeping them. They do, however, serve an additional purpose, that of coupling the U.S. nuclear arsenal with NATO and the defense of Europe.

Without a specific mission for these nuclear weapons, such coupling serves only for long-term reassurance of America's NATO allies. American nuclear weapons that are in Europe do constitute a tangible commitment and add substance to assertions that the U.S. nuclear umbrella continues to protect Europe. There is no certainty that the present threat environment will persist indefinitely. Britain and France have independent nuclear forces, but these are not dedicated to the defense of the whole of NATO as the American weapons are. Germany has no intention of developing its own independent nuclear force and understands the grave political consequences that would follow from such a move. Removal of all U.S. nuclear forces from Europe for the first time since the early days of the Cold War, however, would make a future nuclear Germany more likely than it is now. A small force of about 200 weapons should serve to avoid this outcome. These weapons should be located where they are most secure and easily managed and controlled, even if that means removing them from some countries that would otherwise prefer to keep a few American nuclear weapons on their soil. The weapons would support the flexible response force of 160 weapons carried on the B-2 bombers.

When President Bush inactivated all ground-based tactical nuclear weapons and cut back on other theater nonstrategic weapons, roughly 500 intermediate-range nuclear cruise missiles (submarine- and air-launched) were taken off alert. The capability to deploy these weapons on surface ships was later eliminated, and submarine-launched cruise missiles were placed in a nondeployed reserve status. Air-launched cruise missiles on B-52 bombers remain part of the active force. There is no continuing mission for these nuclear cruise missiles, and they serve no important political purpose, unlike the weapons in Europe.[11] The submarine-launched cruise missiles keep open the possibility that U.S. nuclear submarines might be carrying nuclear weapons and result in denial of some port privileges. Nuclear air-launched cruise missiles add complexity to the B-52 force, which should be converted to a non-nuclear force.

Some analysts have argued that maintaining nuclear weapons at a high state of alert increases the risk of nuclear war.[12] Being on alert, however, can contribute to strategic stability in important ways, and alert status should not be seen as always being negative. The argument against alert status is that forces on hair-trigger alert are likely to be launched based on a false warning of attack. If there is any risk associated with keeping U.S. weapons on alert, it stems from the doctrine that calls for prompt retaliation, which requires a force capable of preemption. If the first-use doctrines related to Europe and damage limitation are eliminated, the prompt retaliatory war plans can be eliminated, and this risk would therefore be eliminated. Further, if the United States eliminates its prompt retaliatory plans against Russia and convinces the Russians through military-to-military and diplomatic contacts that no capability remains to launch a preemptive strike, Russia's incentive to maintain a prompt launch capability should evaporate. This would permit it to eliminate its hair-trigger alert as well. Alert procedures in both countries could be realigned to use alert status strictly to ensure the survivability of nuclear deterrent forces against a surprise attack. Submarine forces on alert are at sea and therefore invulnerable; bomber forces on alert can take off on warning of attack and avoid destruction. Keeping forces on alert in this sense contributes to strategic stability and should be encouraged.

New Threats, New Opportunities

Adopting these changes would not only rationalize U.S. nuclear strategy and posture but would also allow a focus on the most dangerous new threat: the proliferation of weapons of mass destruction to rogue states and terrorist organizations. Meeting these threats requires a mix of military deployments, new arms control approaches, new law enforcement and intelligence community capabilities, and new diplomacy. No amount of military strength will allow America to deal with this new threat alone; a multilateral consensus will be required. Such a consensus can be fashioned only under the strong leadership of the United States but also will require the active cooperation of its NATO allies, China, Japan, and Russia. This cooperation is not likely to be forthcoming unless the United States first changes its strategic vision, nuclear strategy, and force structure along the lines recommended above.

The restructuring of America's strategic nuclear forces proposed here could potentially violate the criterion of "essential equivalence."[13] It is not clear that essential equivalence has any continuing validity as a force planning criterion. But in any event, many experts believe that Russia does not have the capability of maintaining a strategic nuclear force greater than about 1,000 to 1,500 weapons. Thus, even a unilateral restructuring of U.S. forces to that level would preserve de facto parity. Others have argued that any such reduction on the part of the United States should be done only in the context of a negotiated, verifiable arms control agreement. In his West Point commencement speech to the class of 2000, Vice President Al Gore stated,

> An approach that combines serious unilateral reductions with an attempt to build a massive defensive system will create instability, and thus undermine our security. Nuclear unilateralism will hinder, rather than help, arms control. Strategic stability can never be a one-way street. It either exists for both the United States and Russia—or neither. Reductions alone do not guarantee stability—it is how reductions are made and how they interact with defensive systems that makes the difference. That is why arms control and strategic modernization have to be built upon planned and negotiated agreements.[14]

Clearly, there are advantages to obtaining a Russian agreement not to continue an offensive nuclear arms race and to join the United States in reducing forces to 1,200 weapons each. The Russians have already formally proposed in START III negotiations a ceiling of 1,500 strategic weapons, which is a strong indication that such an agreement is possible. Even if an agreed limit of approximately 1,200 weapons is not possible, it is in the interests of the United States to undertake the restructuring recommended here. Explicitly eliminating prompt retaliatory war plans and the de facto first-strike capability they engender and adjusting the force structure accordingly would make it easier to achieve the international consensus necessary to deploy a limited national missile defense (see Chapter 3). This change would also strengthen U.S. diplomatic leverage in nuclear nonproliferation, and most important, permit the president to articulate an understandable and sensible nuclear posture that could obtain a strong domestic political consensus. The Cold War requirements of damage limiting, the nuclear defense of Europe against a Russian invasion, and essential equivalence simply have no continuing validity, and the resulting smaller force is more than adequate for deterrence and other remaining missions.

There are no expansionary or offensive motives that could ever lead an American president to order a nuclear first strike against the military forces of China or Russia and threaten a nuclear holocaust. The first-strike capabilities incorporated into U.S. war plans during the Cold War existed for the defensive missions of extended deterrence and damage limiting. Maintaining these prompt retaliatory attack options—especially if combined with the large national missile defense proposed by many U.S. political leaders and with substantial reductions of the Russian nuclear force that many see as inevitable—could provide a robust first-strike capability if U.S. forces are reduced to the level of 2,500 weapons that the United States has proposed for START III. In contrast, eliminating the prompt retaliatory war plans and reducing the U.S. nuclear force to 1,000 strategic and 200 theater weapons would essentially eliminate the possibility of such a capability, ending the need to convince other nations to rely on the long-term goodwill of the United States rather than on the fact of America's military deployments.

It is arguable that nations complain of America's current nuclear capabilities only to justify their continuation of a confrontation, not because they fail to realize the political impossibility of an American nuclear first strike. Yet the United States has long maintained that actual military capabilities must determine U.S. security policy, not the intentions of potential adversaries. It is hardly reasonable to deny other nations the same viewpoint.

If there were an obvious military or security necessity for the world's remaining superpower, with its overwhelming conventional force dominance, to maintain first-strike war plans and forces, then perhaps other nations could see nonsinister reasons for America's doing so. In the absence of such necessity, these war plans and forces impossibly complicate the diplomatic leadership needed to control the growing threat of weapons of mass destruction—leadership needed both to more rigorously enforce international norms against proliferation and to achieve a new consensus on the acceptable role of ballistic missile defenses in the post–Cold War world.

Notes

1. Radiation Effects Research Foundation, Hiroshima and Nagasaki, www.rerf.or.jp/eigo/faqs/faqse.htm#faq1.

2. See William M. Arkin and Robert S. Norris, "Global Nuclear Stockpiles, 1945–97," *Bulletin of the Atomic Scientists* (November/December 1997), for historic stockpile estimates. Numbers have been reduced since the end of the Cold War. For current deployments, see www.bullatomsci.org/issues/nukenotes/mj00nukenote.html.

3. See www.armscontrol.org/FACTS/statefct.htmal#us.

4. Preempting with nuclear weapons was seriously considered during the 1962 Cuban missile crisis.

5. See www.ait.org.tw/ait/tra.html.

6. See Chapter 4 for a discussion of the arms control context of this move by President Bush.

7. Damage limiting has a better chance of working against China if the damage-limiting attack is preemptive (an unlikely scenario). But not many weapons are needed to perform this mission, since the Chinese have never had more than a few tens of targets.

8. This is true, for example, with regard to North Korea's extensive underground WMD facilities.

9. On a steady-state basis, it is difficult to maintain more than approximately half a strategic ballistic missile submarine fleet at

sea. The other half needs to be in port for crew rotation and training, maintenance of the boats, and occasional overhaul and refueling.

10. Some have argued that single-warhead ICBMs must be retained to permit one-weapon attacks, since SLBMs are all MIRVed. But the proposed B-2 force and 200 theater nuclear bombs are more than adequate if the "prompt retaliatory" war plan is discarded.

11. As discussed above, some useful targeting flexibility could be obtained by configuring the B-2 force to carry a small number of these cruise missiles, but there is no need to maintain the entire B-52 nuclear bomber capability for this limited purpose.

12. Harold A. Feiveson, ed., *The Nuclear Turning Point* (Washington, D.C.: Brookings Institution Press, 1999).

13. See the section on essential equivalence in Chapter 4 for the definition and history of this criterion.

14. See www.usma.edu/class/2000/GradSpeech00.htm.

Chapter 3

Ballistic Missile Defenses

The Origin of Antiballistic Missiles

Each new military technology motivates a search for an effective defense against the newcomer. Large, mounted formations that could quickly invade cities were met with castles and city walls; stronger swords and better arrows motivated steel body armor; machine guns brought about armored tanks and infantry fighting vehicles; and submarines led to sonar and depth charges.

Ballistic missiles have been no exception. As soon as German V-1s began to terrorize Allied cities in World War II (especially London), engineers began to search for an effective defense. By the mid-1960s, advances in radar technology and nuclear miniaturization led engineers to conclude that such a defense was possible. The first major American effort, Nike-X, was derived from the nuclear-armed Nike air defense system. The concept was simple: Powerful, electronic-tracking phased array radars would detect incoming ballistic missile warheads; fast rockets would intercept the warheads outside of or high in the atmosphere; and finally, nuclear explosions would destroy the incoming warheads. In 1967, Secretary of Defense Robert McNamara announced that the United States would deploy a limited version of Nike-X, renamed Sentinel. The mission would not be to stop a Soviet attack, which was beyond the capability of Nike-X. Rather, the system would be focused on the then-emerging Chinese intercontinental ballistic missile threat.

Sentinel was never deployed. Its successor, Safeguard, a reduced deployment of Nike-X components, was dismantled before it was fully operational. Both Sentinel and Safeguard were largely victims of the rapid advances in offensive missile technology that made building an effective antiballistic missile using the Nike-X architecture and technology almost impossible.

Technology Competition: MIRVs and the Demise of ABMs

Perhaps antiballistic missiles could have been perfected against the first generation of ICBMs. The development of multiple independently targetable reentry vehicles in the late 1960s, however, increased the technological challenges facing ABMs by orders of magnitude. As former secretary of defense Harold Brown was fond of saying, "ABMs won't work, and they won't work because MIRVs *do* work."

MIRV technology permits multiple nuclear warheads to be put on a single ballistic missile. By today's standards, MIRVs are a relatively simple technology, but they were revolutionary when they appeared in the late 1960s. Before MIRV technology, a single rocket could carry into space just a single warhead that would be released to follow a gravity-controlled ballistic path to its target. In a MIRVed system, the rocket carries a small automated spaceship called a "bus." The bus carries warheads and various kinds of penetration aids and dispenses them at "bus stops." It maneuvers itself to place each warhead on an independent trajectory and then releases the warhead to follow a gravity-determined ballistic path to its target. Since the bus remains in space only a few minutes before it reenters the atmosphere and burns up, there is a limit to how much it can maneuver and therefore a limit to the "footprint" within which it can drop warheads. But the footprint is large enough to provide considerable targeting flexibility and to force any defense to attack each incoming warhead separately.

At only a relatively small cost to the offense, MIRVs dramatically increase the number of targets an ABM must eliminate to be effective. The largest Soviet rocket, the MIRVed version of the SS-18, could carry ten warheads, forcing an ABM system to shoot down ten times as many targets as it faced with the earlier, single-warhead ICBMs.

The impact of MIRV technology was greater than simply "fractionating" missile payloads. A bus in space also permits dispensing more realistic exoatmospheric (outside-the-atmosphere) penetration aids—usually lightweight balloons whose radar reflections are indistinguishable from those of a live warhead.[1] Large numbers of these decoys can be deployed along with the warheads, vastly complicating the challenge facing the defense. Ground-based radars cannot reliably discriminate between actual warheads and decoys. Either sophisticated sensors would have to be deployed in space, requiring hundreds of orbiting satellites, or the defense must wait until the warheads enter the atmosphere, where the decoys burn up. By that time, only two or three minutes remain to launch short-range endoatmospheric (inside-the-atmosphere) ABMs to thwart the attack. To cover the entire United States with such short-range missiles would require deploying hundreds of them around each potential target (presumably each city or military base). This would almost certainly prove to be infeasible economically, and the defense would still be "leaky," letting at least a few nuclear warheads detonate on American cities.

Even if the exoatmospheric decoy discrimination problem were solved and each ABM system component worked perfectly, building a nationwide ABM system would still be a massive challenge. The efficiency of MIRV fractionation means that it costs ten times as much to destroy a warhead as it does to add one to the offensive arsenal. So, unless the defense can afford to outspend the offense by ten to one, the offense can win in a pure numbers race. Furthermore, MIRVs also facilitate attacks against the ABM defense itself. Many warheads can be concentrated in a nearly simultaneous attack on key elements of the defense, such as the radars that control the ABM system. Processing the data, launching the missiles, avoiding fratricide (one ABM explosion destroying other ABM interceptors), and coordinating in a matter of seconds all the actions necessary to defend the ABM system against tens to hundreds of simultaneously arriving warheads is an almost impossible challenge.

Aircraft or cruise missiles can also be used to attack the radars upon which the ABM system depends. Dealing with these "air breathing, slow flyer" threats presents a challenge comparable to that of defending against incoming missiles. The best air defense rarely destroys more than a few percent of each attacking force (although the United States believes that the B-2 stealth bomber is essentially invulnerable to air defenses). Cruise missiles can be even harder to shoot down. Bomber and cruise missile attacks are much slower than ballistic missiles are and therefore are not useful in a preemptive role, but they can destroy either the ABM system or the targets the ABM was defending.

The ABM Treaty and Nuclear Strategy

ABMs, being defensive systems, are not a direct threat to anyone. Thus, it is difficult to convince some Americans, including many in every Congress elected since ABMs first existed, that there should be any constraints on ABMs. The argument against ABMs is more subtle: They could make impossible the achievement of a strategic equilibrium between adversary powers, and they present technical challenges that make it unlikely they would be effective in stopping a concerted attack.

The 1972 ABM Treaty grew out of this concern over strategic equilibrium and the technical challenges of building an effective defense. The treaty was meant to settle the role of ABMs in nuclear strategy. It did not. Perhaps this was because the Soviet Union strained the terms of the companion Interim Agreement on Strategic Offensive Arms. "Modernization" was permitted under the agreement. But the Soviets "modernized" by completely discarding old missiles and launchers and replacing them with new MIRVed models three times larger. Thus, the 1972 agreements failed to bring the arms race into equilibrium. Whether, as some critics charged, the Soviet deployment of very large MIRVed missiles significantly increased the first-strike threat to America's nuclear deterrent and violated the letter of the Interim Agreement, it certainly violated its spirit. Yet even had the offensive arms race been halted by arms control agreements, the controversy over the proper role of ABMs would likely have continued.

Critics of the ABM Treaty caricatured American strategy as MAD—using the acronym for "mutual assured destruction." These critics argued that with the United States undefended, the large Soviet nuclear force rendered the U.S. nuclear arsenal impotent. Some asserted that by prohibiting ABMs, the United States was permitting the Soviet Union to prevail in a nuclear war. Throughout the Cold War, the United States and NATO relied on the possible first use of nuclear weapons to prevent the overrunning of Europe by Soviet troops. This threat had credibility problems, since the Soviets could respond tit-for-tat to any use of nuclear weapons, causing massive damage to Europe as the war escalated. Some argued that leaving the United States completely undefended against Soviet missiles added insurmountable credibility problems, since it would be clear that no American president would use American weapons first to stop a Soviet invasion with American cities completely unprotected. These critics believed that without the ABM Treaty, the United States could solve the daunting technological problems facing ABM systems, at least well enough to convince the Soviet Union that it would lose an all-out nuclear war. Such knowledge would deter a Soviet nuclear response against the United States should the United States and its NATO allies be forced to resort to nuclear weapons to defend Europe, and would therefore strengthen deterrence of a Soviet attack on Europe in the first place.

European governments relied most heavily on NATO's threat of first use of nuclear weapons for their security. They never seriously attempted to build up their conventional forces to a level that would make the use of nuclear weapons to stop a Soviet invasion unnecessary. They nevertheless opposed U.S. ABM deployments on the ground that a defended United States would become "decoupled" from Europe, preferring to sit out a nuclear war in Europe, and that the Soviets would count on this, making war more, rather than less, likely.

Few advocates of the ABM Treaty favored MAD (or, as it was also caricatured, the "mutual balance of terror") per se. Rather, treaty advocates argued that ABMs simply could never work, which left deterrence as the only mechanism to prevent nuclear war. There is no clear advantage to the United States in deterrence being "mutual"; America's interest is to deter adversaries, not to be deterred by them. Once the Soviet Union developed large forces, however, the dynamics of relations between the two superpowers became another essential consideration in determining the stability of the nuclear balance. If deterrence were not mutual, an arms race would create ongoing tensions, especially if one side saw itself falling seriously behind. The tensions would in turn increase the probability of nuclear war. The ABM Treaty was meant to eliminate this risk by giving both sides confidence in the reliability of their deterrents.

Reagan, SDI, and the End of the Cold War

Notwithstanding these debates, the ABM Treaty remained the cornerstone of Cold War arms control agreements, and the U.S. strategy of relying on deterrence without ABMs remained intact until March 1983, when President Ronald Reagan announced his support of a space-based defense against ballistic missiles. He followed up soon after by announcing the Strategic Defense Initiative (SDI). SDI was a massive attempt to overcome the architectural and technical problems of land-based ABMs by developing a system based on new concepts, such as x-ray lasers and particle-beam weapons. Deployment of the system in space rather than on the ground was a key difference from traditional ABM technology. Basing weapons in space would permit destroying missiles or their bus before penetration aids or warheads were deployed. If a few warheads and decoys were deployed, either lasers or numerous "brilliant pebbles"—small, self-guided interceptors—would destroy them.

After the expenditure of tens of billions of dollars, these efforts have failed to achieve any significant technical success. Many necessary technologies were infeasible; others were either too costly or required decades to develop. Furthermore, deploying a system in space would create a new set of challenges, especially that of the system defending itself against antisatellite attacks. So, the ABM Treaty was left intact—once again—not because there was a consensus in favor of leaving the United States vulnerable to Soviet attack but because no solution could be found to the immense architectural and technical challenges of building an effective nationwide antiballistic missile system.

By the time George Bush succeeded Ronald Reagan, the Gorbachev revolution was well underway in the Soviet Union. START I, signed in July 1991, promised the first real reduction in offensive nuclear arms since the beginning of the Cold War. On September 27 of that year, President Bush announced that as a unilateral initiative the United States would withdraw from service and eventually eliminate all 10,000 of its short-range tactical nuclear missiles. President Gorbachev announced a week later that the Soviet Union would do likewise, although no timetable was promised. By the end of 1991, the Soviet Union had officially ceased to exist. Presidents Bush and Yeltsin agreed to more dramatic nuclear offensive arms reductions in START II, signed in Moscow on January 3, 1993.[2] Once implemented, these actions would reduce Cold War nuclear arsenals by almost 90 percent. With the nuclear arsenals of the two Cold War rivals seeming to collapse overnight, the pressure to erect a magic shield in space disappeared.

Post–Cold War Threats

THE THEATER BALLISTIC MISSILE THREAT

President Bush continued the Strategic Defense Initiative but with a focus on protecting American troops in the field against surface-to-surface ballistic missiles (SSBMs), particularly the growing threat of theater ballistic missiles (TBMs)—longer-range SSBMs, many of which derive from the World War II–era V-2 and its successor, the Russian Scud. Iraqi Scuds constituted the major terrorist threat against the Israeli city of Tel Aviv, especially during the Persian Gulf War in 1991. Several hit Tel Aviv during that war and could have caused high fatalities had they been equipped with the chemical warheads that Saddam possessed but did not use. Concerns that they might be so equipped instigated the distribution of gas masks to Israeli citizens and threatened the escalation of the war by motivating Israel's retaliation against the Scuds.

The theater ballistic missile threat against the cities of U.S. friends and allies is only the most dramatic manifestation of the proliferation of ballistic missile technology. The more urgent threat is against U.S. and allied troops. Iraq's Scuds were responsible for half the U.S. combat casualties in the Gulf War when a single Scud hit the U.S. airbase in Dhahran, Saudi Arabia, killing 27 Americans and wounding 98 others.[3] Until the Intermediate-Range Nuclear Forces (INF) Treaty of 1987 eliminated all shorter-range U.S. and Soviet ballistic missiles, these weapons represented a major threat to NATO forces. By the early 1990s, there were more than 30 countries with TBM programs. In response, the United States joined with other nations to create the Missile Technology Control Regime (MTCR) in an attempt to stop the spread of TBMs.

TBMs are only a limited threat when used with conventional warheads (although not a trivial one, as evidenced by the successful Iraqi attack on the Dhahran air base mentioned above). Even the V-2s did relatively little damage to London. They are an inaccurate and inefficient way to deliver conventional ordinance when compared to bombs, air-launched missiles, and artillery. But TBMs are a major threat when equipped with WMD warheads. Since there are essentially no effective defenses against them today, a WMD warhead delivered by a TBM can be highly lethal to unprotected troops or civilians.

RESPONDING TO THE TMD THREAT

Efforts to give air defense systems a capability against TBMs have been underway for decades. During the Persian Gulf War, the Patriot Advanced Capability (PAC) air defense system was rushed to the Gulf to protect troops and Israeli cities. But it proved ineffective against even the crude Scud threat of Saddam. Immediately after the war, President Bush accelerated efforts to give the Patriot at least a modest capability against TBMs, and noncombat tests indicate that the PAC-2 is in fact improved. A completely new version, the PAC-3, should begin to enter service soon.

Both the Bush and Clinton administrations have put a major effort into a family of new TMD systems—the army's Theater High-Altitude Area Defense system (THAAD), the navy's Area Defense and Theater-Wide systems, and the air force's Airborne Laser. Limited work has also been done jointly with NATO allies on a mobile short-range system with capability against aircraft, cruise missiles, and ballistic missiles—the Medium Extended Air Defense System (MEADS).

These systems will play a major role against emerging WMD threats. For many countries, they could form the basis for national defenses against ballistic missiles. Japan and Taiwan are both close enough to China that either the U.S. Army THAAD or the U.S. Navy Theater-Wide will be able to intercept any Chinese ballistic missile attack against them. Likewise, threats against much of Europe from Iran, Iraq, or even former Soviet states could be intercepted by systems that are technically TMD systems. Using its own and American TMD technologies, Israel is developing its Arrow system to protect itself against threats from the Middle East.

The refocus of ABM technology development on TMD also opened a diplomatic challenge for the United States. The ABM Treaty limited only national missile defenses and imposed no constraints on defenses against shorter-range tactical or theater ballistic missiles. In 1972, such missiles hardly existed, and there were no good concepts for how to defend against the ones that did. As a result, negotiators saw no reason to complicate the ABM Treaty negotiations by attempting to develop a rigorous definition establishing the "demarcation" between national missile defenses and theater missile defenses. As TMD systems were developed in later years, none of the early technologies offered any capability at all against strategic missiles—they could not intercept a strategic warhead in the easiest possible circumstance, a one-on-one engagement. With the advent of more capable systems, such as THAAD and U.S. Navy Area Defense, demarcation questions became more difficult, since these systems, especially if coupled with space-based sensors capable of "cueing" the interceptor, could potentially destroy strategic warheads in a one-on-one engagement. Nothing in the ABM Treaty indicated that a system had to pass the test of no capability in a one-on-one engagement. But, like the Miranda warning, which was initially established by the courts as a "sufficient" warning to meet the constitutional test and later, for convenience, became accepted as a "necessary" warning, meeting the "no one-on-one capability" test became accepted by some executive branch lawyers as a necessary test.[4] Russian officials also began to question the more sophisticated U.S. TMD programs such as the THAAD and navy Theater-Wide systems. Thus, efforts began to negotiate a rigorous demarcation agreement to supplement the ABM Treaty, making clear which systems were permitted and which were not.

These efforts were finally successful in March 1997, when Presidents Clinton and Yeltsin committed to a demarcation agreement at their Helsinki summit. Secretary of State Madeleine Albright and Foreign Minister Yevgeny Primakov signed the text of the agreement in New York the following September, and the Russian Duma ratified the changes at the same time that it ratified START II on April 14, 2000.[5] The U.S. Senate has yet to ratify the change. The agreement defines a "safe harbor" for antiballistic missiles with terminal velocities of less than three kilometers per second and prohibits TMDs—that is, defines them as NMDs covered by the treaty—if they are tested against a missile with a range greater than 3,500 kilometers or with a terminal velocity greater than five kilometers per second. Missiles not tested as prohibited but with a velocity faster than the safe harbor rule are subject to analysis by the deploying country to determine whether the system can threaten the strategic force of the adversary—not merely the capability to hit a single warhead in a one-on-one engagement.

Perhaps the greatest significance of the history of the TMD demarcation negotiations is what it illustrates about the importance of rethinking arms control agreements as technologies and international politics change. The ABM Treaty was completed at a time when there were no WMD threats from smaller powers and no serious TMD technology possibilities. Today the situation is radically different. Even now, after completion of the TMD demarcation agreement, the issue remains. The Republican leadership in the U.S. Senate has refused to consider ratification of the changes necessary to put the demarcation agreement in effect, perhaps more because of its desire to see broader changes in the ABM Treaty than because of any problems with the demarcation agreement itself. But as the United States decides how to respond to the ballistic missile threat against the cities of its friends and allies and its troops overseas, the diplomatic effects of TMD decisions will be inseparable from those of ABM decisions, especially in Asia.

NEW ROGUE STATE THREATS

Both Russia and the United States thought that the TMD demarcation agreement would settle the ABM Treaty issue for the foreseeable future. The joint statement issued by Presidents Clinton and Yeltsin and the formal agreement completed five months later reemphasized the importance of preserving the ABM Treaty and its essential role in maintaining nuclear stability. The Clinton administration did not anticipate the refusal of Senator Jesse Helms to permit the agreement to be considered for ratification. But even if it had been ratified, the TMD demarcation agreement would not have settled even the near-term future of the

ABM Treaty. In 1998, the Rumsfeld Commission reported that a new threat not previously the focus of ballistic missile defense programs had arisen.[6] Both Iran and North Korea were developing long-range ballistic missiles with the potential to attack portions of the United States. Iran appeared to be at least several years away from even testing a long-range missile and, unlike North Korea, was not thought to have access to a nuclear weapon. The immediate threat came from North Korea, which had already tested a long-range Taepo Dong I missile and produced enough plutonium to manufacture one or two nuclear weapons before its nuclear weapons program was frozen by the 1995 Agreed Framework.

Today, the citizens of the Democratic People's Republic of Korea (DPRK) are starving, their government has stopped testing of long-range missiles as a result of the Perry process,[7] and a diplomatic thaw is underway with South Korea. Nevertheless, North Korea continues to devote significant efforts and technological prowess to missile programs. With a concerted effort, it can probably cobble together a low-reliability missile that could deliver a 700-kilogram warhead to the West Coast of the United States with enough capacity to carry a crude nuclear device. The U.S. intelligence community has estimated that the North Koreans could field an operational system within a short time after successfully testing its next generation missile, the Taepo Dong II. The moratorium could be broken without notice and a crude operational system fielded perhaps as quickly as two years thereafter.

North Korea is spending a significant portion of its tiny gross domestic product on developing an ICBM, apparently assuming that success will bring it additional prestige and sales of its technology to other rogue states attempting to acquire weapons of mass destruction. It has relied heavily on exports of missile technology for foreign exchange and probably sees the development of a longer-range missile as important to its prospects of future arms sales. Perhaps it believes that it will eventually be able to field a large enough nuclear and ballistic missile force to become a significant world military power. Finally, it may believe that these weapons can give it leverage against the United States, and it perhaps hopes to drive American troops out of South Korea and force a settlement with South Korea on terms favorable to itself.

None of these motives portends an actual attack, which would bring a devastating response and eliminate the DPRK regime. The North Koreans seem to understand that they cannot prevail in a military confrontation. In 1994, North Korea's refusal to halt plutonium production led to a U.S. conventional force buildup that compelled it to back down. It was deterred from mounting its threat, just as it would be if it attempted nuclear blackmail with a crude ICBM. But the Taepo Dong II represents the first direct threat against the American homeland since Russia and China developed their ICBMs during the Cold War. Leaving it unchallenged would be politically unthinkable. Likewise, should Iran or Iraq continue with efforts to develop nuclear weapons and ICBMs to deliver them against U.S. territory, the threat would have to be met, either by direct military action to eliminate it or by defending against it if at all possible. Protracted containment and deterrence would never be a politically acceptable response to such threats in the United States.

RESPONDING TO THE ROGUE STATE THREAT

In the summer of 1999, the Clinton administration announced acceptance of congressional demands that it set a firm date of 2005 for the initial operational capability of a national missile defense. This represented a major change in NMD policy from a focus on development to setting a date for deployment. The system the administration chose starts with a first phase of 100 ground-based interceptors in Alaska that are capable of defending the entire nation, including Alaska and Hawaii, from a few tens of North Korean warheads. A phase II program would include an additional 100 interceptors deployed by 2010 in the center of the country. Phase II would be capable of defending against tens of warheads accompanied by more complex penetration aids from either North Korea or the Middle East.

In 1999, President Clinton attached conditions to his deployment commitment and stated that he would make a final decision in 2000. On September 1, 2000, he announced that the conditions had not been met, so that the beginning of construction would be delayed until the next president, inaugurated in January 2001, could reach his own decision on deployment. Clinton stated that the key reason for the postponement of a deployment decision was the need for further technical development and testing. Only one of three key flight tests had succeeded, and important components were behind schedule. A full system test using the new radar and new booster rocket is some time away, and the effectiveness of the key component, the exoatmospheric kill vehicle (EKV), is far from proven. The EKV is the final stage of the interceptor rocket, which maneuvers to hit the approaching warhead directly and destroy it on impact. It has yet to be demonstrated that the EKV can intercept a warhead surrounded with even simple realistic decoys, and some experts doubt that it will ever do so.[8] Furthermore, some required commitments from other countries (radars will be required in the United Kingdom, for example) have not yet been obtained. The president suggested also that more time could be used to work out differences with Russia on the ABM Treaty.

The 1999 announcement that a national missile defense would be deployed to meet the emerging North Korean threat once again brought forth all the questions that have been debated since the 1960s: technical feasibility, strategic wisdom, cost, and alliance politics. This time, however, the context is radically different: The Cold War is over, China is a rising power, and the threat against which the system is ostensibly to be deployed comes from a backward, bankrupt, small power that is holding out with its Stalinist dictatorship against the rest of the world.

President Clinton's postponement of the anti-DPRK NMD was favored by almost all interested parties. Immediate deployment of the proposed system was opposed by a majority in Congress and defense experts in both political parties. Further, it would have set off a diplomatic clash with Russia, China, and Europe. The current design, which is unlikely to be ready on schedule given its poor test record, is too limited to satisfy strong advocates of a national missile defense. Even some who support NMD prefer to sort out current diplomatic challenges prior to its deployment, given the impossibility of obtaining the consent to ABM Treaty revisions from Russia and two-thirds of the U.S. Senate before the required notification date. Without this consent, America's abrogation of the ABM Treaty would be inevitable, which would threaten the entire arms control regime built during the Cold War.

The projected North Korean nuclear force would have no effective military capability. A North Korean attack would be a terrorist attack against innocent civilians. With at most two warheads, an inaccurate missile that could miss by several miles, and uncertain reliability, North Korea could harm U.S. military capabilities only by pure luck. The nature of its threat is terrorist rather than military. If the deterrence of such a terrorist threat is thought inadequate, the defense should be effective against all methods of delivering a terrorist weapon. The proposed NMD system leaves unopposed several other delivery means—for example, bringing a ship into a major American harbor, using a disguised aircraft, or deploying a simple cruise missile. Assuming that North Korea has one or two nuclear warheads available, an effective ABM would deprive North Korea of only the most flashy and psychologically intimidating attack mode but not of its ability to threaten or undertake a nuclear attack on the United States.

Fortunately, historical evidence indicates that the North Koreans are rational enough to be susceptible to deterrence. This was evidenced most recently from the 1994 experience, mentioned above, of North Korea backing down and completing the Agreed Framework in the face of a U.S. conventional force buildup of relatively modest proportions. Further, it is abiding by the testing moratorium negotiated by Perry and making increasing progress in its negotiation of a new relationship with South Korea. There seems to be little justification for a crash program to deploy an ABM system that would add little confidence to the already high U.S. ability to meet a North Korean threat. There is no reason not to proceed in a considered and prudent fashion.

A New Strategic Concept for Ballistic Missile Defenses

The United States needs a new strategic concept for dealing with ballistic missile defenses, not just a quick fix to deal with a possible North Korean threat. This policy must deal with the technological, strategic, and diplomatic challenges that ABMs pose, while acknowledging their potential contribution to the security of the United States and its allies.

This new strategy should begin with the reality that an SDI-like "shield" is impossible. It is probably impossible to perfect the technology necessary to stop today's generation of ballistic missiles anytime in the foreseeable future. Yet even if it were possible, the program would motivate a response from adversaries that would inevitably offset the defense. More sophisticated penetration aids, larger numbers of MIRVs, attacks on the defense itself, cruise missiles, more bombers, and antisatellite weapons are all technologies that could offset a nationwide defense against a sophisticated enemy. While there is no adversary capable of mounting such responses today, an American attempt to build an airtight national missile defense, in the face of America's nuclear superiority and overwhelming conventional military dominance, would strongly motivate nations and coalitions to respond.

The impossibility of a shield against all attacks does not mean that ballistic missile defense should be abandoned. There are five important strategic missions for limited defenses:

1. Theater missile defenses are needed to protect U.S. troops in the field and the cities of U.S. friends and allies.

2. While the chance of accidental launch is low, a direct defense would provide insurance against such an occurrence.

3. If deterrence fails against a state such as North Korea, Iran, or Iraq (if it succeeded in developing nuclear missiles), a direct defense can protect the United States. There is always the possibility of these states disintegrating, with

their nuclear weapons falling into the hands of terrorists or an unstable leader who might not be deterred.

4. A defense might help deter the development by rogue states of an ICBM capability by making clear that the United States will not tolerate such a threat.

5. Finally, a limited national defense, even if it can intercept only a few warheads (twenty-five to fifty), can enhance deterrence in a crisis by making it necessary for an adversary to launch a relatively large nuclear attack to overcome the defense. Intimidation by threatening one or two nuclear missiles is eliminated. A crisis is therefore less likely to escalate to war in the first place.

This last strategic mission is perhaps the most important. An attack that grows out of a diplomatic crisis is the most likely threat to the United States homeland—greater than the risk of an accidental or surprise attack. In the midst of such a crisis, when each step the United States takes runs the risk of leading to a WMD attack, a national missile defense would have a significant benefit by increasing the U.S. freedom of action. By forcing a large attack to penetrate or destroy the defense, a national missile defense raises the stakes for a potential attacker and thereby gives American leaders considerably more flexibility to act in a crisis. An American leader might be prepared to act under the protection of a limited national missile defense despite a threat of nuclear retaliation, even knowing that the retaliation could ultimately overwhelm the U.S. defense. An adversary would understand that the relatively large attack required to defeat even a limited American ABM system would risk overwhelming retaliation from the entire U.S. nuclear force.

Providing this freedom of action is also important in facing threats from a rogue state, a terrorist group, or a rogue officer in a nuclear state who gains control of even a single missile. The more immediate benefit would be to make it clear that the United States retains freedom of action. This knowledge alone will deter most rogue states, terrorist groups, and individuals from attempting either blackmail or an attack. (Some potential proliferators might decide to abandon their WMD program altogether in the face of a U.S. NMD.) Since any potential defense will be imperfect, preventing the attack is a dramatically better strategy than relying on the defense to intercept it after launch.

The end of the Cold War, combined with Russia's difficulty in adapting to a market economy, has eliminated any chance that a reasonable ABM deployment will trigger a preemptive nuclear war or an offensive nuclear arms race between Russia and the United States. Yet these are the main scenarios that the ABM Treaty and its prohibition of national missile defenses were intended to deal with. It should be possible to negotiate a cooperative regime permitting the United States to adopt a new strategy that includes limited ballistic missile defenses.

New Technology for a New Strategy

Today, such a strategy cannot be implemented because the technology is not available. The United States cannot even carry out the first and most basic BMD mission of providing effective TMDs to defend American troops in the field. The first true TMD, PAC-3, which is a modification of a thirty-year-old design, is not scheduled for deployment until 2002. The first new-generation system, the Theater High-Altitude Area Defense system, or THAAD, is scheduled for 2007. The navy's Theater-Wide system is a decade away. The Medium Extended Air Defense System, or MEADS, and the air force's Airborne Laser are not even programmed for deployment.

Even when these systems are deployed, they will have many weaknesses. The current designs are pieced together from a variety of programs developed by the three military services, each with its own unique capabilities focused on the mission of the service developing it rather than on supporting joint warfare. Furthermore, design compromises have been made to accommodate outdated ABM Treaty provisions. In the future, new architectures and technologies, some of which are discussed below, can improve significantly on these first generation TMDs. But it would be a mistake to stop work and redesign them now. These systems will provide valuable operational experience and be able to handle the most common ballistic missile threats, most of which are variants of the Russian Scud, which is in turn a variant of the World War II German V-2 rocket. The current designs are not so seriously flawed that deployment should be delayed.

A key technology for all future ballistic missile defenses is "hit-to-kill." A nonnuclear explosion is unlikely to destroy an incoming warhead, especially outside the atmosphere. Interception is most efficiently accomplished by hitting the target directly using a hit-to-kill vehicle that homes in on a ballistic missile warhead or booster rocket in flight. The missile and interceptor travel toward each other at such a high closing velocity that tremendous kinetic energy is released in a collision.

Developing better hit-to-kill technology in a small package is important for both TMD and NMD systems. Miniaturizing means that more hit-to-kill vehicles can be deployed on an interceptor or, as proposed in the "brilliant pebbles" concept, as autonomous weapons in space. Hit-to-kill technology deserves separate emphasis and should be developed independently of the platform carrying the hit-to-kill vehicles.

Present designs for a limited NMD system are based on "traditional" ABM architecture, consisting of ground-based radars to detect and track incoming warheads and ground-based interceptor missiles to destroy the warheads. This is still the most feasible architecture for intercepting warheads launched from Russian ICBM bases against the United States, although space-based detection and tracking of warheads can play an important role. But for emerging threats such as North Korea, Iran, and Iraq, completely different technologies offer significant advantages. In particular, "boost-phase" technologies potentially could solve both technological and diplomatic problems raised by traditional architectures.[9]

In a boost-phase BMD, the missile is destroyed during its powered flight. Stopping ICBMs in their boost phase before they "fractionate" into MIRVs and deploy their penetration aids may be the only reliable ABM technology, given the tremendous advantage decoys have over decoy discriminators. Boost-phase intercept requires fast identification and fast rockets or lasers to catch an in-flight ICBM.

In addition to having the great advantage of negating penetration aids, boost-phase systems have military and diplomatic advantages. Militarily, they are equally useful against theater ballistic missiles or ICBMs. Air-based or sea-based systems could be deployed as TMDs or against a rogue state threat as an NMD. Diplomatically, boost-phase systems offer the advantage of not threatening the strategic forces of Russia or China. Both Russia and China have large land areas that permit deploying their ICBM forces in areas not reachable by U.S. boost-phase systems, and Russia has a significant submarine-launched ballistic missile force that would not be affected.

The main disadvantage of boost-phase systems is that the interceptors must be deployed near the launch sites. Theoretically, boost-phase interceptors could be based in space. But for the foreseeable future, they must be deployed on land, in aircraft or drones, or on ships. Each of these platforms presents some challenges and vulnerabilities. Aircraft and drones are obviously vulnerable to air defense systems, and present ships (Aegis guided-missile ships) do not have the necessary equipment, in addition to being extraordinarily expensive assets to leave on station indefinitely. Land-based deployment requires access to nearby bases from third countries that may not grant it.

It is a considerable challenge to design and develop a workable boost-phase approach. Operational systems are probably a decade away at a minimum. Some have suggested that upgrading the Standard missile on existing Aegis guided-missile ships would provide a quick solution to such threats as the North Korean Taepo Dong II. Aegis radar, however, cannot both track the target and guide the interceptor at the same time, and a faster missile will not fit into the Standard missile launchers. A sea-based boost-phase system requires an entirely new program—a new (or rebuilt) ship, new radar, a new missile, and a new command-and-control system. This could cost $50 billion, depending on how many ships are dedicated to this task and how much protection the ships need. Development and deployment of such a system would take at least a decade. It may well be worth the cost, since the existing Aegis/Standard system will always have serious limitations. There is no fast or inexpensive method of obtaining sea-based boost-phase TMD.

Boost-phase systems could add to U.S. TMD capabilities, and they could handle most rogue state ICBM deployments. But they are not a panacea. Two elements of the proposed strategy for ballistic missile defense, insurance against accidental launches and enhancing deterrence of Russia or China in a crisis, still require a limited direct defense of the United States, which for the foreseeable future would have to be built around the traditional architecture of radars and interceptors. Such a system using the 100 interceptors permitted by the ABM Treaty could provide this capability. It would be important to deploy a worldwide space-based warning and tracking system to enhance the other NMD technologies included in such a system, and the interceptors would have to be deployed at multiple sites to protect the entire United States. Both of these elements would require major changes to or abrogation of the ABM Treaty—a consideration discussed in the following section.

In addition to these technologies, air defense must receive increased attention. Otherwise, a rogue state desiring to threaten the United States has the easy option of deploying WMD on aircraft or cruise missiles. Perhaps integration of civilian air traffic control with military surveillance of the continental United States and the development of reliable identification systems for all authorized aircraft based on military "identification friend-or-foe" (IFF) systems would be the most useful steps. Transmitting authentication signals encrypted with the same public key encryption technology that makes Internet commerce feasible can be done inexpensively and reliably. An improved air defense system would eliminate the current easy option of flying an unknown aircraft that carries a terrorist or rogue-state weapon into U.S. airspace, which is an option rogue states with nuclear weapons would certainly attempt to develop if they faced an effective U.S. ABM system.

Stopping maritime threats is also important. Today, no capability exists to track or inspect more than a small portion of the thousands of boats and ships arriving in U.S. harbors each day. Deterrence, intelligence, and traditional law enforcement methods are the only available defenses against maritime WMD threats, whether they emanate from state actors or terrorists. New technologies may eventually be able to help register and track all arriving boats and ships and detect some types of WMD on board. But, just as is the case with narcotics and contraband, the rapid increase in international trade will make a direct defense against WMD smuggling increasingly difficult.

ABM Diplomacy

Perfecting TMD systems, designing and developing workable boost-phase systems, and redesigning a 100-interceptor limited ground-based system will take considerable time. If the United States announces a new strategy for ballistic missile defense that is not a threat to nonhostile powers and makes clear that this strategy will be pursued consistently, it should be possible to develop a cooperative approach that would be widely accepted.

The first step in gathering support to change the Cold War paradigm is changing the U.S. nuclear strategy and force structure. The previous chapter explained how throughout the nuclear age the United States has relied on the capability of mounting nuclear weapons first in a crisis. It recommended giving up this capability, except in the few limited cases of attacking the isolated state or terrorist WMD target that threatened the United States, its friends, or its allies. There are good strategic reasons that are independent of ABM considerations to abandon the "prompt retaliatory" war plans that result in a de facto first-strike capability against Russia and China. Doing so is necessary if the United States is to forge a diplomatic consensus that supports the inclusion of limited ABMs in a new regime of deterrence and cooperation.

Dropping the prompt retaliatory strikes from the SIOP would permit a reduction of the U.S. nuclear force to 1,000 strategic weapons and no more than 200 theater-based weapons in Europe. Such a small number would constitute a credible first-strike force only if it were accompanied by a large ABM deployment such as the Global Protection Against Limited Strikes (GPALS) system discussed below. But the more limited U.S. ABMs recommended would be threatening to other powers only in combination with larger offensive nuclear forces. Other powers will accept limited ABM deployments only if offensive forces are also limited. Adopting policies that do not presage absolute military dominance is therefore necessary both to avoid the formation of coalitions opposing the interests of the United States more broadly and to permit successful deployment of a limited ABM system to meet the missions set forth above.

Moving to smaller "no-first-strike" offensive nuclear forces simultaneously with deploying limited national missile defenses (based on a combination of boost-phase and traditional land-based technologies) contrasts with both the recent efforts to negotiate START III reductions and ABM Treaty modifications. In recent negotiations, the United States has held out for *higher* numbers of offensive weapons in START III (2,500 warheads versus 1,500 proposed by Russia) while asking for changes to permit 100 interceptors now and more later in an NMD system. Such a combination is simply too close to permitting the United States a de facto first-strike capability to be acceptable to Russia or to China and other major powers not directly involved.

The approach recommended here also contrasts with the GPALS approach apparently favored by George W. Bush. GPALS would involve 1,000 interceptors plus space-based "brilliant pebbles" interceptors combined with very low levels of offensive nuclear forces. Portions of the system would be offered to other nations. GPALS represents a move to "defense dominance" and away from reliance on nuclear deterrence. The other nuclear powers will not trust their ability to deploy air-tight defenses and therefore will not give up their nuclear deterrents.

President Putin has rejected proposals to modify the 1972 ABM Treaty while hinting that there are ways to protect all of Europe, including Russia, and the United States from missile threats without violating the ABM Treaty. The Russian plan likely involves some form of boost-phase intercept capability and thus should not oppose that aspect of the recommended strategy. But until a new approach to the offense-defense nuclear relationship is worked out, Russia will oppose changes to the ABM Treaty. A STRANSS treaty that replaces both START and the ABM Treaty could reflect such a revised offense-defense relationship and would therefore have a better chance of succeeding than attempts to modify the ABM Treaty without reconsidering the broader context. In Chapter 4, this arms control approach is discussed in greater detail.

Sharing ABM technology would be an important aid to U.S. ABM diplomacy. Many proposals exist for the United States to share its ABM and TMD capabilities with other countries. Giving all friendly nations the ability to use a common space-based ballistic missile detection and tracking system would build support for limited defenses as part of a new strategic balance. (The new joint missile early warning center of the United States and Russia announced at the June 2000 Moscow summit is an important move in that direction.) Such a system would permit adding small numbers of interceptors essentially anywhere in the world to provide the same benefits the United States would receive from an ABM system. Eliminating the threat of WMD delivered by ballistic missiles will not eliminate all WMD threats, but it could force rogue states and terrorists to take more difficult routes if they persist in using WMD to achieve their objectives.

A new policy on ABM defenses must be integrated with alliance relations and broad foreign policy objectives. NATO and the alliance with Japan remain particularly important to U.S. security, as do relations with Russia and China. A national missile defense program that ignores these relationships could reduce rather than enhance national security.

NATO must be comfortable that it has a path to an effective defense against potential Iranian and Iraqi WMD threats. Mobile boost-phase systems could provide a significant portion of any such defense. Maintaining the American nuclear umbrella over Europe and a strong transatlantic conventional defense relationship are also important. Keeping 200 U.S. air-delivered theater nuclear weapons in Europe should be adequate tangible evidence of a continuing nuclear link. Maintaining both patience with and support of NATO as the European Defense Program is implemented should cement the nonnuclear defense relationship. In return, the United States can reasonably expect rigorous support for nonproliferation efforts and greater financial contributions toward developing the theater ballistic missile defenses necessary to protect NATO forces in battle.

Asia presents a greater challenge to U.S. ABM-related diplomacy. The United States maintains a nuclear umbrella over Japan as part of its security commitment to that country. This nuclear commitment serves to reassure a nonnuclear Japan that it can remain nonnuclear without fear of either nuclear attack or nuclear blackmail. As Korea reunifies and China continues the slow but deliberate improvement of its nuclear and conventional military capabilities, Japan will have to participate more in maintaining the security equilibrium in Asia. Many flash points could lead to war in Asia. North Korean desperation, a breakdown between Taiwan and mainland China, civil collapse in Indonesia, anarchy in Cambodia, and drug wars in Thailand and Burma are some of the possibilities.

Japan will increasingly want protection against ballistic missiles from North Korea and China. Taiwan wants protection from PRC missiles, such as those launched in the direction of Taiwan during the confrontational exercises of 1996.[10] The ballistic missiles most likely to threaten Japan or Taiwan are theater range missiles, not intercontinental range missiles. Theater missile defense systems, rather than the national missile defense systems needed by the United States, are necessary to counter them. The United States is already sharing TMD technology with Japan and has provided a version of the PAC-2 system to Taiwan. U.S. mobile sea-based and air-based boost-phase intercept systems could be made available in a crisis, but a significant indigenous BMD capability is likely to be important to both Japan and Taiwan if China continues with its buildup.

China has complained loudly about the prospect of American TMDs protecting Taiwan. China opposes all U.S. military assistance to Taiwan as a violation of the normalization communiqués. The United States could provide TMD technology to Taiwan on the grounds that China should not have increased its ballistic missile threat in the first place and that the TMD system has no offensive role. China might respond by asserting that the Taiwanese TMD serves the offensive role of protecting Taiwan against mainland retaliation should Taiwan attack. The only solution satisfying all parties is progress with the reconciliation between Taipei and Beijing to the point where no perceived threat remains to Taiwan. In the short run, China needs to halt its ballistic missile buildup, which threatens Taiwan as well as other neighbors. The United States should continue to limit TMD cooperation to the existing PAC-2 derivative program for a few years. This would give diplomacy time to work both with China and between the mainland and Taiwan. The United States should make clear to China that enhanced TMD technology will be provided to Taiwan should China continue to increase its ballistic missile threat to the island.

China has no legitimate reason to threaten Taiwan or Japan militarily, and the United States has a commitment to ensure that neither Taiwan nor Japan is attacked. Nevertheless, providing theater missile defense capabilities to Japan, Taiwan, and possibly a unified Korea might, if seen as a threat by China, motivate China to stimulate another round in an offense-defense arms race in Asia. Likewise, the deployment of a thin United States missile defense, as recommended here, could motivate the Chinese to expand their ICBM force. Even the limited 100-interceptor force recommended above would have the capability to intercept today's Chinese ICBM force, largely eliminating China's nuclear deterrent. China would also worry that in a Taiwan crisis, a U.S. NMD would eliminate whatever negotiating strength it obtains by being a nuclear power. China can move to MIRV its ICBMs, creating a greater crisis stability problem unless the ICBMs are made mobile and invulnerable, or simply add to its force.

The United States will likely be faced with gradual increases in Chinese nuclear capabilities as the new strategy for ballistic missile defense is implemented over the next decade or so. Such an improvement is probably inevitable in any case, as a result of the growth in Chinese economic strength and technological capabilities. Modest increases, from today's level of about 25 warheads capable of reaching the United States to 100 to 200 warheads, will not change the strategic balance or represent a significant additional threat to the United States. Moreover, these increases would be large enough to ensure penetration of the limited 100-interceptor NMD recommended here. Likewise, China might expand and improve its force of short-range ballistic missiles, which are capable of hitting targets in the region, including Russia, from today's level of about 300 to 500. Such an expansion will be unwelcome, but to make it a casus belli would be a mistake. U.S. diplomacy should anticipate such expansions. The U.S. ability to deter a Chinese attack against Japan, South Korea, Taiwan, or itself would not be affected by increases of this level, and a limited direct defense for Japan, Taiwan, and the United States is worth the result of moderately expanded Chinese nuclear forces.

It will take a decade or more to develop a workable national missile defense that can carry out all five missions set forth above. Hopefully, nonthreatening but effective mobile boost-phase technology can be perfected, along with new shared space-based warning and tracking and effective ground-based launchers for a 100-interceptor NMD. Meanwhile, if the United States takes the steps recommended here to restructure its nuclear policies and forces, a new international consensus can be forged on the role of defenses in the strategic balance. Doing so could reduce tensions with both Russia and China and perhaps assist in their progress toward becoming the democratic states that the United States wants them to become. If such a transition occurs, both states might see less reason to maintain a nuclear deterrent against the United States. Russia and China would therefore be less concerned that a limited U.S. national missile defense threatens them, easing any tensions brought about by America's deployment of an NMD. Moreover, if Russia and China become more fully integrated into the community of democratic states, they will act more forcefully to stop the proliferation of WMD, further strengthening the regime of cooperation.

Notes

1. William J. Broad, "Antimissile Testing Is Rigged to Hide a Flaw, Critics Say," *New York Times*, June 9, 2000.

2. See www.ceip.org/programs/npp/factsheet1.htm.

3. William Claiborne, "SCUD Kills 27 GIs at Dhahran Billet," *Washington Post*, February 26, 1991.

4. This experience demonstrates the hidden risks of taking the easy way out in policy debates. Throughout most of the history of the ABM Treaty, there was no possibility of a TMD interceptor hitting a much higher and faster ICBM in a one-on-one engagement. Everyone agreed that an interceptor with not even a one-on-one capability was not covered by the treaty, so this easy test was used. But the mere precedent of using the test led the lawyers to refuse to abandon it when technology rendered the judgment required more complex.

5. See cns.miis.edu/pubs/reports/start2.htm.

6. India has also undertaken a slow but steady development of longer-range missiles, and Japan's space launchers could theoretically deliver warheads to intercontinental ranges. But neither country is a threat to the United States.

7. In 1999, former secretary of defense William Perry, acting as President Clinton's special envoy, negotiated a moratorium in the North Korean missile development program in return for relaxation in U.S. economic sanctions.

8. William Broad, "Antimissile Testing," *New York Times,* June 9, 2000.

9. A focus on boost-phase architectures was first proposed by Dean A. Wilkening, *Ballistic-Missile Defence and Strategic Stability,* Adelphi Paper 334, International Institute for Strategic Studies, London, May 2000, and more recently elaborated in John Deutch, Harold Brown, and John P. White, "National Missile Defense: Is There Another Way?" *Foreign Policy* 119 (Summer 2000), pp. 91–99. See also Richard Garwin, "Boost-Phase Intercept: A Better Alternative," *Arms Control Today* 30, no. 7 (September 2000), pp. 8–11.

10. See collegian.ksu.edu/v100/n113/ap-taiwan-china-18.html.

Chapter 4

Nuclear Arms Control

While almost every type of weapon has been subject to constraint through negotiated arms control, the focus of arms control has been on weapons of mass destruction. Since World War II, the most pressing arms control objective has been to reduce the risk of nuclear war. Nuclear arms control has been the centerpiece of nearly every summit between U.S. and Russian leaders, a major diplomatic issue with NATO allies, and the subject of frequent and sometimes strident public debate. Despite political, diplomatic, and technical challenges, four major sets of nuclear arms control agreements have been successfully concluded:

- The Strategic Arms Limitations Treaties and the more recent Strategic Arms Reduction Treaties set limits on the types and numbers of strategic nuclear weapons possessed by Russia and the United States.

- The 1972 Antiballistic Missile Treaty effectively prohibits ballistic missile defenses of the territory of both the former Soviet Union and the United States.

- The Limited Test Ban Treaty, the Threshold Test Ban Treaty, and the Comprehensive Test Ban Treaty have placed ever-tighter constraints on testing nuclear devices.

- The Nuclear Nonproliferation Treaty and its associated institutions prohibit nonnuclear states that are parties to the treaty from developing or acquiring nuclear weapons.

Important multilateral supporting institutions have been developed to control the spread of WMD technology, including the Wassenaar Agreement, the Zangger Committee, the Australia Group, and the Missile Technology Control Regime. These institutions focus on regulating the flow of "dual-use technology"—technology that has legitimate nonmilitary uses but that can also be used to develop weapons of mass destruction. Their primary benefit is to define potentially dangerous exports and enhance the transparency of a state's export control efforts through reporting and monitoring regimes.

Taken together, these agreements create a complex arms control regime regulating nuclear weapons. This regime has set important norms against WMD proliferation, and it most likely has slowed the proliferation of nuclear weapons—in the 1950s, many observers predicted that there would be 25 or more nuclear powers by the end of the century.

Early Arms Control Efforts

These efforts at arms control began almost immediately after nuclear weapons were developed. The Baruch Plan proposed the multilateral control of all nuclear weapons. Several scientists proposed eliminating all existing weapons and banning them forever by international agreement. Their military utility seemed to be huge, however, and the complications of verifying a ban or creating a workable international institution to control them seemed insurmountable. So it was that the first serious nuclear arms control agreement was not reached until 1963, when President John Kennedy completed negotiations with the Soviet Union on the Limited Test Ban Treaty that prohibited the atmospheric testing of nuclear weapons.

The Limited Test Ban Treaty removed a significant atmospheric pollutant, but it had no substantial effect on the development of nuclear technology. It was not until 1972 that the first nuclear arms control agreements were reached that had a perceptible effect on the actual deployments of the two superpowers.

Controlling the Arms Race by Limiting ABMs

The 1972 Antiballistic Missile Treaty and the Interim Agreement on Strategic Offensive Arms were bilateral agreements between the United States and the Soviet Union. They had the ambitious goal of establishing agreed-upon principles for maintaining strategic stability between the superpowers. By that time, both sides had built very substantial strategic offensive forces, large enough to destroy each other. The leaders of both nations knew that nuclear war was not winnable, and they seemed prepared to live with deterrence to ensure their safety. Antiballistic missile defenses nonetheless threatened to upset the strategic balance and motivate another round of offensive arms buildups.

One of the many ironies of nuclear strategy is that any plausible threat to a nation's nuclear deterrent must be met with a vigorous response. The stakes are so high that no uncertainty about one's ability to retaliate effectively, and thus to deter the attack in the first place, can be tolerated. Both the United States and the Soviet Union came to understand this principle early in the nuclear age. They realized that an effort by one side to deploy a national missile defense could very well lead to a disproportionate increase in the other side's offensive forces, even if the chances were low that the national missile defense would work as hoped. Thus, if an NMD competition ensued, it might become impossible to control the arms race. Yet without some control of the arms race, a reduction of the ideological conflict that drove the East-West confrontation in the first place seemed impossible.

JOHNSON AT GLASSBORO

President Lyndon Johnson had approved the deployment of the Sentinel ABM system in 1967, focused not on the Soviet Union's missile threat but on the newly emerging Chinese ICBM threat. Johnson understood that deploying an ABM defense against the Soviet Union might well lead to another round in the arms race, after an expensive competition in defenses. The U.S. defense budget was already terribly strained, and inflation was increasing because of the deficit financing of the Vietnam War. Johnson was under pressure from powerful national security leaders in Congress not to leave the nation "undefended." The decision was made to deploy a limited defense against China, a power that was just emerging as a threat. Russia was told that the system was not a threat to its deterrent, and in any case, it was well along on its own defense systems, Galosh and Tallin.

When skepticism of both the cost and technical feasibility of even the limited Sentinel system mounted in Congress, Johnson decided to engage the Soviets in an effort to negotiate a settlement of the nuclear arms race. Near the end of his term, he met briefly with Soviet Premier Aleksei Kosygin at Glassboro College in New Jersey to start the process. The Nuclear Nonproliferation Treaty was just being completed, which added momentum to the concept of using negotiations to reduce the risk of nuclear war.[1]

NIXON'S CONTROVERSIAL 1972 AGREEMENTS

A few months later, President Richard Nixon took office and began an immediate review of both the Sentinel program and the Johnson-Kosygin talks. Nixon's national security adviser, Henry Kissinger, believed that a negotiation was feasible. In fact, he felt it was a necessary component of the détente policy he hoped to pursue with the Soviet Union. Kissinger also felt that without a deployed ABM system the United States would be at a severe disadvantage in the negotiations, given the Soviets' rapid progress in deploying its Galosh ABM around Moscow and apparent efforts to give the widely deployed SA-5 Tallin air defense system a capability against ballistic missiles. The result was to revise the Sentinel program, cutting back its size and changing its mission from one of defending against China to that of defending American ICBM bases against a possible Soviet attack. The new system was named Safeguard. Its deployment was barely approved by the U.S. Senate, Vice President Spiro Agnew having to break a 50-to-50 tie to avoid defeat.

Some worried that an ABM arms race was now under way. Nixon and Kissinger's real purpose in pushing for the deployment of Safeguard was to motivate the Russians to agree to a comprehensive arms control regime, freezing both the offensive and the defensive nuclear force deployments and opening the way for broader political détente. As a result, soon after the Safeguard vote, Nixon and Kissinger opened the Strategic Arms Limitation Talks (SALT) with the Soviets. Both sides acknowledged the technological impossibility of building a nationwide ABM and the resulting necessity of relying upon nuclear deterrence rather than direct defense. These principles were enshrined in the 1972 ABM Treaty.[2] Shortly thereafter, Secretary of Defense James Schlesinger convinced President Nixon to deactivate the Safeguard ABM system. This was done primarily to save money, but it was also because Safeguard's contribution to America's deterrent was small in any case.

Since the purpose of the ABM Treaty was to bring about a stable strategic equilibrium between the rival superpowers, the United States insisted throughout the SALT negotiations that any ABM agreement be accompanied by an agreement on offensive nuclear arms. The result was the 1972 Interim Agreement on Strategic Offensive Arms. The Interim Agreement was meant to freeze the deployment of the offensive arms of each side while a more permanent treaty was negotiated.

With the completion of SALT I—as the ABM Treaty and Interim Agreement together came to be called—arms control agreements played an increasingly important role in determining the composition and size of U.S. and Soviet strategic and nuclear forces. SALT I stopped ABM deployments and froze the number of missile launchers. However, since MIRVed missiles were the most efficient way to increase nuclear firepower and could be deployed in existing launchers ("silos"), the capability of the two forces continued to grow. Furthermore, SALT I permitted the modernization of land-based ICBM launchers. The Soviets used flexibility in the agreement's definition of "modernization" to increase the total capability of their offensive nuclear force by a factor of three or more. They did this by blowing up the old missile silos and replacing them with new and stronger silos that were 52 percent larger and by using a "cold launch" technique. This permitted a much bigger missile, one that could carry as many as six warheads in the case of the SS-19, which replaced the single-warhead SS-11. This was far from the intended "freeze" in offensive forces. SALT I had failed to bring about a new equilibrium, but it did bring the ABM race to a halt for more than a decade.

Essential Equivalence

The follow-on SALT II agreement and the subsequent START talks initiated during the Reagan administration were structured to control directly the number of deployed weapons, which is a better measure of force capability than is the number of launchers. SALT I had also locked in a small Soviet advantage in the number of strategic nuclear delivery vehicles (the total of missile launchers and bombers). With some relatively minor exceptions, SALT II and all subsequent treaties contained numeric limits that were the same for both sides.

Essential equivalence and equal aggregates became the guiding principles for strategic offensive arms agreements and therefore for nuclear force structures. As discussed in Chapter 2, there is no military or strategic rationale for these concepts. They are not based on the missions assigned to nuclear weapons, nor do they account for the many variables that determine the effectiveness of a nuclear force. Their rationale was political: How could

U.S. allies or the American public be confident in the U.S. deterrent if the Soviets had a larger number of launchers or weapons?[3]

The basic outline of SALT II had been agreed upon during the Ford administration at the Vladivostok summit. After an initial false start, the Carter administration resumed the negotiations and completed the treaty, agreeing on equal aggregates—that is, equal numbers of strategic delivery vehicles and MIRVed ICBMs. The December 1979 Soviet invasion of Afghanistan, however, effectively brought a halt to arms control negotiations between the superpowers. President Jimmy Carter had submitted SALT II to the U.S. Senate for ratification, but after the invasion the treaty was withdrawn. It was never ratified, although both sides continued to abide by its limits.

Focusing offensive arms control on countable items—strategic delivery vehicles, launchers, and warheads—and requiring that the numbers be identical for each side had the unintended effect of turning what were supposed to be maximum allowable limits into de facto minimum deployment levels. The levels set in SALT II were close to the maximum level in each category that either side planned to reach. The agreement codified these plans and stopped intelligence officers from predicting even larger numbers, which might have resulted in a further upward spiral in deployment levels. The reality was that by this time—with about 10,000 nuclear warheads in each nation's arsenal, each warhead averaging about twenty times the yield of the Hiroshima bomb—there was not much appetite for further quantitative increases and even some sympathy for reducing numbers. But once negotiators accepted the political necessity of having equal numbers of everything, it became impossible for either side to unilaterally reduce its forces below the established limits.

The Strategic Defense Initiative

President Ronald Reagan came to office with no sympathy for the arms control process. In March 1983, he announced a radical shift in U.S. strategic policy and programs. Henceforth the United

States would focus its efforts on building an impenetrable shield in space against ballistic missile warheads. His Strategic Defense Initiative was completely at odds with the tacit agreement between the superpowers reached in 1972 with the ABM Treaty. It would turn the offense-defense relationship on its head—replacing offense dominance with defense dominance.

The offense has enough inherent advantage in a nuclear exchange that pure numbers can eventually overcome virtually any conceivable defense. Thus, part of the process of moving from offense dominance to defense dominance is to obtain the lowest possible limits on offensive forces. Reagan and his team therefore decided early on to renounce the Strategic Arms Limitation Talks approach of limiting aggregates to equal numbers and to insist on true reductions. Thus, in 1982 they dramatically renamed the negotiations as the Strategic Arms Reduction Talks. The talks reached a turning point at the October 1986 summit between Presidents Gorbachev and Reagan in Reykjavik, Iceland. A tentative agreement was reached to eliminate all ballistic missiles on both sides in ten years, but Gorbachev insisted on a reaffirmation of the ABM Treaty's prohibition of national missile defenses. This would have meant the death of Reagan's treasured SDI.

START was not completed during Reagan's eight-year term. There was, however, a major arms control accomplishment a year after Reykjavik: the Intermediate-Range Nuclear Forces Treaty. The INF Treaty called for the elimination of all U.S. and Soviet nuclear-capable land-based missiles (ballistic and cruise) with ranges between 500 and 5,500 kilometers. It grew out of the Soviet buildup of intermediate range missiles aimed at Western Europe and NATO's response of deploying Pershing and improved Lance missiles. As a result of the agreement, the Soviets destroyed 1,846 missiles and the United States destroyed 846 missiles. The treaty did not affect the nuclear balance or the strategies or capabilities of either side. Furthermore, many thousands of longer-range missiles, shorter-range missiles, and aircraft-delivered weapons, all related to the NATO–Soviet Union nuclear confrontation in Europe, were not covered by the agreement. Still, the treaty was significant in several respects:

- For the first time, the two sides moved away from equal aggregates. The organizing principle of the treaty was the "zero option"—getting rid of an entire class of weapons.

- The weapons involved would have facilitated fast escalation to nuclear war in Europe, the most likely nuclear war scenario. Eliminating them reduced this risk somewhat.

- On-site inspections and extensive data sharing were incorporated for the first time in a major arms control agreement.

The First Post–Cold War Decade

ELIMINATING TACTICAL NUCLEAR WEAPONS

In December 1989, the Berlin Wall fell. A year later the Soviet Union abandoned its geopolitical ally, Iraq, and participated alongside the United States in the Persian Gulf War. On July 30, 1991, Presidents Bush and Gorbachev signed START I, which reduced strategic weapons by several thousand on each side to 6,000 "accountable" weapons, roughly a 30 percent cut. Acknowledging the revolutionary change underway, President Bush in the fall of 1991 took an extraordinarily bold step in announcing the unilateral abandonment of 90 percent of America's deployed nonstrategic nuclear weapons.[4] A few weeks later, President Gorbachev reciprocated by announcing similar steps.[5] He also proposed a START II agreement that would result in a cut in strategic nuclear forces of 50 percent from START I levels, down to one-third of the Cold War levels. Then, on December 24, 1991, the Soviet Union ceased to exist.

Whether or not Russia completes its promised reciprocation of America's elimination of short-range nuclear weapons, there is no reason to consider reintroducing them into American forces or strategy. A tactical nuclear war in Europe never was likely to give

NATO a true military advantage. Soviet retaliation with short-range weapons would have killed tens of millions of Western European citizens, destroyed major cities, and decimated NATO conventional military units. Nonetheless, Europe felt it necessary to make this threat because of perceived inferiority in conventional forces.

Today, NATO's conventional forces are vastly superior to those of Russia. Russia no longer has available the forces and buffer zone of the Warsaw Pact. Poland, Hungary, and the Czech Republic are full members of NATO, and all the other former Warsaw Pact nations would certainly side with NATO rather than Russia in a European war. With such an overwhelming conventional advantage for NATO, there is little chance that Russia would undertake a conventional war against Western Europe, no matter how dramatically the Russian political system might change. Neither a resurgent communist movement nor a nationalist movement in Russia could change these facts. As a result, Russia's remaining short-range nuclear weapons provide no useful strategic advantage, even if Russia continues to delay their destruction. An attempt on Russia's part to use tactical nuclear weapons against Western military forces would result in retaliation by American, British, and French strategic forces and America's European-based air-delivered theater nuclear weapons. Meanwhile, NATO's conventional forces would probably quickly overwhelm and defeat Russia's conventional forces. The difficulty Russia faced in subduing a few thousand ill-equipped Chechnya freedom fighters illustrates how much Russian military capabilities have deteriorated.

REDUCING START LIMITS TO 2,500 WARHEADS

START II was signed by Presidents Bush and Yeltsin in January 1993, just before President Bush left office. It reduced strategic weapons from 6,000 "accountable weapons"—which worked out to 7,000 to 8,000 actually deployed weapons—to 3,000 to 3,500 actually deployed weapons. Quite open inspection and data exchange provisions promised to make the venture highly cooperative, although the big shift in this regard had occurred with the INF and START I treaties.

The 1993–94 Nuclear Posture Review conducted by the Clinton administration reconsidered all aspects of America's nuclear posture in light of the end of the Cold War and the dramatic arms control progress underway.[6] The Nuclear Posture Review, however, went no further than to ratify the decisions made by the Bush administration to accept a reduction to 3,500 strategic nuclear weapons in START II. It also reiterated traditional criteria for sizing and structuring nuclear forces: crisis stability, deterrence of a Russian preemptive attack, damage limitation, and extended deterrence for allies. Much focus was placed on the possibility of a resurgent Russia. Meanwhile, the United States kept its forces at START I levels, presumably in order to leverage Russia's ratification of START II. This policy was codified into law in 1997.[7] Russia has also kept its forces notionally at the START I level, although budgetary limitations have rendered many of its forces inoperable.

Gridlock

As the Clinton administration ends and President Vladimir Putin establishes his new administration in Russia, arms control efforts to deal with WMD proliferation seem to be gridlocked:

- START II, signed by President Bush in the last days of his administration, languished for seven years before recently being ratified by Russia. Russia's ratification was linked to U.S. ratification of 1997 changes to the ABM Treaty demarcating the difference between permitted theater ballistic missile defenses and prohibited national missile defenses. But the chair of the Senate Foreign Relations Committee, Jesse Helms, has asserted that he will use his power to block ratification of ABM Treaty changes, so the Clinton administration did not even submit the necessary protocols to the Senate.[8]

- Notwithstanding the delay in bringing START II into force, Presidents Clinton and Yeltsin at their Helsinki summit in March 1997 agreed to negotiate even deeper reductions in a subsequent START III agreement—down to a level of 2,000 to 2,500 weapons. Russia has since proposed even lower numbers, but U.S. negotiators have demanded as a condition for lower numbers Russia's agreement to modify the ABM Treaty to permit immediate construction of a limited missile defense against North Korea and possibly Iran. Russia, on the other hand, has stated that it will accept no modifications to the ABM Treaty and will withdraw from all nuclear arms control agreements if the United States violates or abrogates the treaty. NATO allies have expressed serious concerns about U.S. policy on ABMs and the ABM Treaty.

- The Comprehensive Test Ban Treaty, seen by many diplomats as a central element of U.S. efforts to curb nuclear proliferation, was successfully negotiated in 1996. But its entry into force was conditioned on India's and Pakistan's acceptance of the treaty, and both countries not only refused to accept the treaty but violated its terms when they began nuclear testing in 1998. Then, in 1999 the U.S. Senate voted against ratification. Many countries have reduced their willingness to cooperate with the United States on arms control because of America's failure to ratify the CTBT.

- The Chemical Weapons Convention was completed in January 1993 and subsequently signed by most of the world's nations. Its enforcement arm, the Office for the Prevention of Chemical Weapons (OPCW), however, is only partially operational because the U.S. Senate has blocked full implementation of OPCW's right to inspect American facilities.

- The United States places the highest priority on bringing China into compliance with WMD nonproliferation norms. But China has threatened to halt cooperation on nonproliferation matters, including its participation in the Missile Technology Control Regime, if the United States provides theater ballistic missile defenses to Taiwan or proceeds with a national missile defense—both steps the United States is poised to take.[9]

The United States and Russia each finds itself in the bizarre position of professing a strong commitment to arms control but threatening to drop out of the Cold War arms control regime if the other does not agree to changes it wants to see made. The United States threatens to abandon the ABM Treaty, the foundation of the Cold War arms control regime, unless it is substantially modified to permit active defenses against new post–Cold War ballistic missile threats. Russia wants even lower limits on offensive forces in START III but threatens to abandon the offensive agreements altogether if the United States withdraws from the ABM Treaty in order to deploy a defense against North Korea and Iran. In both Russia and the United States, there is significant parliamentary opposition both to changing the regime and to leaving it unchanged.

This arms control gridlock has been attributed to many factors: President Yeltsin's inability to control his Duma; President Clinton's fights with the Republican Congress; America's decision to deploy a national missile defense system; and weak diplomacy on both sides. The fundamental cause of the gridlock, however, is the breakdown of a consensus on underlying principles to guide the arms control process. A consensus was reached in 1972 when the principle of maintaining nuclear stability through assured retaliation was accepted by both the United States and the Soviet Union and reflected in the SALT I agreements. There have been many steps taken by each side that are inconsistent with this principle, but it has nonetheless remained the most important agreed-upon principle throughout the Cold War. When the principle was threatened, most notably by President Reagan's SDI program, arms control came to a halt.[10]

Today, Russia sees the combination of U.S. military dominance and the deployment of a national missile defense as a threat to this principle, and arms control is once again blocked. The United States asserts continued acceptance of the principle and argues that the changes needed in the ABM Treaty to accommodate a limited national missile defense do not threaten the principle. America's actual deployments and war plans can be read otherwise. Likewise, Russia's rhetoric and some of its deployments (particularly its retention of a large tactical nuclear weapons force almost a decade after promising to eliminate it) are inconsistent with the principle of limiting nuclear missions to deterrence through assured retaliation.

Breaking the gridlock that stifles efforts at WMD risk reduction was not an accomplishment of President Clinton; it will fall to the new U.S. administration. Presidents Clinton and Putin were unable to settle arms control matters at their June 2000 summit, although they did agree to continuing negotiations on the ABM Treaty and informal discussions on further offensive reductions in START III. Knowing that a new government would probably revise U.S. policy, however, Russia was increasingly reluctant to reach agreements with the Clinton administration. Furthermore, ratification of new protocols or agreements by the U.S. Senate, a remote prospect all along in light of Senator Helms's categorical statements, became increasingly unlikely as the administration wound down. The result was to defer the decisions needed to move the process forward to the new president.

A New Nuclear Arms Control Regime

PRINCIPLES GUIDING A NEW REGIME

Chapters 2 and 3 set forth a new post–Cold War strategy and force structure for America's strategic weapons and for a possible future national missile defense. Chapter 2 also recommended a new nuclear force structure, reducing America's nuclear arsenal to 1,200 weapons from a Cold War high of more than 25,000. Announcing this new force structure and beginning the multiyear process of moving to it would add significant credibility to the declaration of a new strategy of deterrence and cooperation.

After making such an announcement, the United States should enter into negotiations with Russia with the goal of replacing both START and the ABM Treaty with new arms control agreements that reflect this new strategy and force structure. The following principles should guide these negotiations:

1. While neither allies nor partners, the United States and Russia are no longer enemies. Changing U.S. strategy by dropping "prompt retaliatory" war plans against Russia and reducing strategic warheads to 1,000, both of which have been recommended here as sensible on their own merits, would acknowledge this momentous shift. In the distant future, perhaps the two nations could move toward a nuclear relationship such as the United States, Britain, and France have, seeing no threat whatsoever to one another. Many more changes would be needed on Russia's side, including comparable strategic and tactical nuclear weapons reductions, dramatic improvements in safety and security, retreating from its first-strike doctrine and preparations, and completion of its transition to a stable democracy. Meanwhile, there will be a benefit in regulating the nuclear forces of the two sides through arms control agreements, but the agreements should reflect the end of the Cold War ideological confrontation.

2. The next round of nuclear arms control should focus less on mandating reductions in the number of weapons, since both sides want reductions with or without arms control, than on strategic transparency, safety, and stability (STRANSS).

    -   *Transparency:* The many data and test notifications and on-site inspection rights included in the SALT, START, and INF treaties, and the institutions that exercise these rights, should be consolidated and strengthened. Nuclear risk reduction centers (NRRCs) can play an ever-increasing role in this process.

    -   *Safety:* Keeping nuclear weapons and nuclear materials out of the hands of unauthorized individuals, states, and terrorist organizations is fundamental. It should be a commitment of each nation. Making this a treaty commitment will eliminate excuses for unsafe conditions, such as inadequate budgets or bureaucratic resistance. If Russia is willing to make such a commitment, the United States should respond by increasing significantly the amount of technical and financial aid it provides through the Cooperative Threat Reduction (CTR) program.

- *Stability:* The new agreement should ban first-strike war plans and deploying first-strike capabilities. It should mandate that each side deploy invulnerable weapons, so as not to tempt a first strike. It should acknowledge that a limited NMD can add to strategic stability.

3. A STRANSS treaty should leave each side the flexibility to structure its nuclear forces. There should be complete "freedom to mix" various weapons types. Any numeric limits should be warhead aggregates, including all deployed nuclear weapons, regardless of their range or delivery mechanisms. Open inspections can eliminate the need for constraints that were imposed during the Cold War primarily because of verification concerns. START II's prohibition of MIRVed land-based ICBMs was an attempt to reduce instabilities in the balance of forces—MIRVed ICBMs constitute relatively attractive targets for a first strike. This prohibition was always of limited value, but the United States has no need for land-based MIRVs, so there would be no damage done in keeping it. Keeping a few MIRVed ICBMs might save Russia some money, so Russia might ask that the ban be dropped. If so, there is little reason to trade off more valuable aspects of the agreement to save it.

4. STRANSS should establish a new strategic offense-defense relationship and replace the ABM Treaty as well as START. It should preserve the prohibition against large national missile defenses, but permit a light national missile defense against new threats and small attacks. Several alternative

methods are available for defining such a limit. The easiest would be to retain the current ABM Treaty limit of 100 ground-based launchers, while dropping constraints on the number of deployment sites, radars, and space-based sensors. Alternatively, the agreement could set a quantitative "performance" limit prohibiting a capability to intercept more than fifty incoming warheads accompanied by sophisticated decoys. This approach is directly linked to the objectives of the treaty but harder to verify because of the uncertainties inherent in the performance of any ABM system.

THE NUCLEAR NONPROLIFERATION TREATY

The Nuclear Nonproliferation Treaty has been the backbone of America's nuclear nonproliferation strategy. It was first signed in 1968 and was extended to indefinite duration in 1995. The NPT not only prohibits the acquisition of nuclear weapons by nonnuclear signatories of the treaty, but it also prohibits the transfer of nuclear weapons technology by nuclear weapons states to nonnuclear weapons states. Since the end of the Cold War, all states except India, Israel, and Pakistan and the five declared nuclear powers have renounced plans to develop nuclear weapons and have joined the NPT. Brazil, Argentina, Taiwan, South Korea, and South Africa all had nuclear weapons programs during the Cold War but have now renounced them. South Africa had built an operational arsenal of, according to its own statements, seven nuclear weapons. It has announced that these weapons have been destroyed, although no outside third party has verified either the destruction or the South African claims regarding the size of the arsenal.

The NPT was the first significant multilateral arms control agreement that included built-in enforcement provisions. The NPT created an international organization, the International Atomic Energy Agency (IAEA), which is responsible for monitoring nuclear facilities of nonnuclear states party to the treaty. This monitoring is designed to ensure that no "peaceful" nuclear activities are used covertly to develop nuclear weapons. The IAEA model became the basis (with many differences in details) for the enforcement provisions later included in the Chemical Weapons Convention and proposed for the Biological Weapons Convention.

It is important to understand the NPT for what it is worth, acknowledging what it can and cannot accomplish. The NPT will not lead to the elimination of nuclear weapons, despite the provisions of Article VI calling for nuclear abolition (nor will it lead to general and complete disarmament, also called for by Article VI). The NPT has not been able to stop all proliferation—India, Israel, and Pakistan refused to join so they could develop their own nuclear weapons. The NPT's enforcement arm, the IAEA, cannot prevent a determined covert program. North Korea and Iraq joined the NPT, but both countries successfully carried out covert nuclear weapons programs under the nose of the IAEA. The NPT has also motivated considerable foot-dragging by nonnuclear states. These states have used the Article VI call for nuclear disarmament to criticize the nuclear states and to justify their covert nuclear programs. India, Pakistan, and Iran have been the most voluble of those states in this regard. Others have made use of the inherent contradiction between Article VI and the policies of the nuclear weapons states to gain rhetorical points in diplomatic forums such as the U.N. General Assembly.

But the NPT has one crucial achievement—it has established an accepted international norm against transferring nuclear weapons technology from nuclear weapons states to a nonnuclear state. After the Cold War, the NPT became the mechanism by which states that had equivocated about nuclear weapons could make a legally binding commitment to forego them. When Iraq and North Korea were caught cheating, the NPT became the rallying point for an international consensus to insist on compliance. When China and Russia were caught orchestrating (or at least condoning) prohibited exports of nuclear technology to rogue states, the NPT allowed the United States and its allies to raise the diplomatic stakes substantially and insist that the leakage be stopped. The NPT should remain the centerpiece of U.S.

nonproliferation diplomacy, despite its weaknesses and contradictions. It should be strengthened, not undercut.

In strengthening the NPT regime, India and Pakistan present special problems. Pakistan will remain nuclear as long as India is nuclear, and India will remain nuclear as long as China is nuclear—which might be forever. India first detonated a "peaceful nuclear explosion" (i.e., a nuclear bomb) in 1974, so it has been a de facto nuclear power for a quarter of a century. But its decision to declare and test its nuclear weapons, highly popular with India's voters, eliminates the option of ambiguity concerning its intentions. Nuclear testing did the same for Pakistan.

Having two declared nuclear powers that are highly unlikely to roll back their nuclear programs leaves the NPT in a state of limbo. It is supposed to regulate the spread of nuclear weapons throughout the world, which is clearly impossible with two nuclear powers outside the treaty. It is not clear what rules govern them—are they bound by the export controls and commitment to work against further proliferation imposed by the NPT or not? To date, India has not been a major source of WMD proliferation assistance, but India has done much less than is possible to help solve the WMD problem. Pakistan has extensive nuclear-related commerce with China, North Korea, and possibly Iran.

The NPT would be stronger with both India and Pakistan admitted as nuclear weapons states, a position completely contrary to current U.S. policy.[11] A new "line in the sand" would be drawn at seven versus five nuclear powers. The situation would be different from 1968 when the NPT was signed because all major states other than the five acknowledged nuclear powers have made a pledge to remain nonnuclear by joining the NPT. The issue of who would be permitted by the international community to have nuclear weapons would be settled. Any state that refused to join the consensus could be treated as a rogue state and isolated. (Israel would remain ambiguous, but as discussed below, there will come a time when Israel must give up nuclear weapons.)

Notwithstanding the logic of bringing both India and Pakistan into the NPT, doing so will remain diplomatically infeasible for the foreseeable future. Their admission as nuclear weapons states would require obtaining the unanimous consent of the parties to the treaty, an almost impossible task. Many nations (including the United States) believe that it would be a major mistake to "reward" India for its proliferation by bringing it into the regime or to reward Pakistan for resisting the years of diplomatic pressure against its nuclear program. Others would remain concerned that admitting India and Pakistan would open the possibility of admitting other states that are today nonnuclear should they change their policies, such as Japan or Germany, notwithstanding the existing treaty commitment of all such states to remain nonnuclear.

For the moment, the best compromise would be for the United States to acknowledge openly India's and Pakistan's nuclear status and insist that they live by the nonproliferation provisions of both the NPT and its supporting institutions, even though they are not members. Both nations could be admitted to some of the supporting institutions (such as the Wassenaar Agreement or the Zangger Committee) if they agree to their strict provisions on technology transfer. Both states should be strongly pressured not to develop "hair trigger" nuclear weapons delivery systems. They each have land-based missile programs that could easily motivate a preemptive strike during a crisis. These programs should be rolled back. Finally, both states should be given whatever assistance is possible consistent with the NPT's prohibitions on technology transfer to improve their nuclear weapons safety, security, and control.

Israel has not and probably will not acknowledge its nuclear weapons program. Very strong historical and ideological reasons will prohibit Israel's giving up its program until there is a secure peace in the Middle East. When peace comes, there will be no further reason to keep it; Israel's conventional military dominance will be adequate for its security. In the interim, the ambiguity will remain the only option.

Perhaps the most important step related to the NPT would be to strengthen the capabilities of the IAEA. The improvements in intelligence cooperation recommended in Chapter 6 would help considerably. The recent challenge-inspection procedures, put in place in response to failures in Iraq and North Korea, must be implemented vigorously. Finally, the parties to the NPT must take a more realistic view of the limits of the IAEA. The IAEA can only indict; it can never give a state a clean bill of health. It will remain up to the member states to find hidden proliferation and to organize the international community to take action against the offending state.

THE COMPREHENSIVE TEST BAN TREATY

The Comprehensive Test Ban Treaty is supposed to slow the nuclear arms race by making it more difficult for nuclear weapons states to expand their arsenals with newer, more capable weapons. Furthermore, to stop testing, it is argued, would make nuclear weapons progressively less reliable, reducing the chance that they would ever be used. In this manner, the CTBT would serve as tangible evidence that the nuclear weapons states were serious about their commitments under Article VI of the NPT to eventual nuclear disarmament. It would become harder and harder to maintain nuclear stockpiles, and eventually nuclear weapons would have to be given up altogether because replacements could not be reliably developed. The CTBT has, not surprisingly, been strongly advocated by those who support a strategic vision of nuclear abolition.

The 1999 CTBT ratification debate offers another example of the inconsistencies inherent in U.S. nuclear policy. The Clinton administration accepted the rationale for the treaty explained above. But when the treaty was submitted for ratification, the administration reaffirmed its strong commitment to nuclear deterrence and the maintenance of a strong nuclear force. Administration officials insisted that the treaty would not interfere with maintaining a strong U.S. nuclear deterrent into the indefinite future. Weapon safety and reliability would be ensured through the "stockpile stewardship program" (SSP), based on computer simulations advertised as being as good as testing itself. Critics of the treaty were therefore able to raise the obvious question of the treaty's purpose. The original argument that a CTBT would eventually force nuclear disarmament had apparently been overtaken by the technological breakthrough of the computer simulations that formed the basis for the SSP (which carried the relatively high cost of $4 billion per year). The computer simulations would essentially be testing by other means.

The CTBT was intended to affect only the five declared nuclear weapons states, since nonnuclear states party to the NPT were already prohibited from any nuclear weapon–related activities including testing, and it was hoped that all nonnuclear states would join the NPT. As it became increasingly clear that India and Pakistan would not join the NPT, there was hope that they would sign the CTBT. Agreeing to forego testing would have kept them as undeclared nuclear weapons states, which was presumably an advantage in controlling proliferation.

The U.S. failure to ratify the CTBT has affected other nations' willingness to cooperate with the United States on issues related to WMD proliferation. States argue that by refusing to agree to give up its nuclear testing, the United States is both violating its Article VI NPT pledge and perpetuating its military dominance. Ratification of the treaty would have the benefit of eliminating this complaint, although it would not bring the treaty into force. By its own terms, the treaty cannot go into effect until India signs. India has used U.S. failure to ratify as an excuse not to sign the treaty, so if the United States were to ratify it, India might eventually sign. Pakistan would likely follow, which would stop further testing in South Asia—a positive development, although certainly not a major impediment to the nuclear programs of either state.

The United States needs to eliminate the CTBT ratification issue as an impediment to its broader WMD control strategy. The worst approach to the CTBT is for the U.S. executive and legislative branches to continue to have conflicting approaches. Yet without a clear tangible benefit to ratification, it will be difficult to obtain Senate consent since it will be many years before at least one-third of the Senate is no longer composed of individuals who voted against the CTBT in 1999. India's joining would be such a benefit. (Pakistan has pledged to join if India does.) A reasonable compromise would be for the United States to link its willingness to reconsider CTBT ratification to India's signing the treaty first, rather than allowing India to say that it will decide what to do only after the United States ratifies. India has already made an ambiguous commitment to sign if the United States ratifies, so this should not be impossible to negotiate. India could agree to ratify concurrently with the United States. The net effect would be India and the United States each conditioning their ratification on ratification by the other, ensuring for both states that they would not be a party to the treaty without the other. With the benefit of India's and Pakistan's participation, U.S. ratification should be possible. The SSP has made progress since 1999, so some of the technical concerns expressed in the last debate should also be reduced.

Notes

1. The NPT was signed in 1968, and the Glassboro summit took place June 23, 1967.

2. The treaty allowed two sites of up to 100 launches each. A 1974 protocol reduced the limit to a single site.

3. Paul Nitze argued throughout this period that aggregate throw weight of missiles also had to be equal. Others argued that aggregate megatonnage of nuclear yield had to be equal. Jan M. Lodal, "Assuring Strategic Stability: An Alternative View," *Foreign Affairs* 54, no. 3 (April 1976), pp. 462–81.

4. These roughly 10,000 weapons consisted mostly of short-range tactical weapons, such as nuclear artillery, and longer-range air-delivered weapons not covered by the INF Treaty.

5. Russia has moved slowly in implementing this pledge but continues to assert that it plans to follow through as budgetary and practical constraints permit.

6. See www.dtic.mil/execsec/adr95/npr_html.

7. *National Defense Authorization Act for Fiscal Year 1998,* H.R. 1119, Public Law 105–85.

8. The 1997 protocols also included changes to START II, adjusting dates to reflect the delay in its implementation.

9. John Pomfret, "China Threatens Arms Control Collapse," *Washington Post*, July 14, 2000, p. A1.

10. The Russians walked out of START and the INF negotiations in December 1993 in protest against NATO's INF deployments, but their strong opposition to SDI had been behind deteriorating relations.

11. Strobe Talbott, "Dealing with the Bomb in South Asia," *Foreign Affairs* 78, no. 2 (March/April 1999), pp. 110–22.

Chapter 5

Enforcing Chemical and Biological Weapons Abolition

Humankind has suffered from weapons of mass destruction for centuries. Biological weapons date at least from the Middle Ages, when soldiers threw the bodies of bubonic plague victims over the walls of enemy cities in an attempt to kill enough residents to force the cities to surrender.[1] The invention of chemical weapons came later, but they have been used much more extensively. Their initial use was geared toward causing great confusion and panic among enemy troops before an assault. On the eastern front during World War I, the Germans rained a barrage of gas-filled artillery shells on Russian troops on January 3, 1915. This was followed by a breakthrough in the war thought to be decisive. In the west, the Germans initiated the first large-scale gas attack on April 22, 1915, at Langemark, Belgium, resulting in a five-mile-wide cloud of chlorine gas.[2] Within thirty minutes, the French army suffered 15,000 casualties and 5,000 fatalities. The age of modern chemical warfare had begun.

By 1918, one out of every four artillery shells fired in the war contained a gaseous agent. World War I saw over one million casualties and one hundred thousand deaths related to chemical weapons.[3] As depicted by John Singer Sargent in his painting *Gassed,* many of the surviving soldiers were left blind or permanently scarred from the blistering effects of chemicals. Among the casualties was Adolf Hitler, then a corporal in the German army, who was temporarily blinded during a British gas attack in Flanders. His personal suffering at the hands of these insidious weapons may have influenced his decision not to deploy them on the battlefield during World War II.

The psychological impact of the indiscriminate and ghastly nature of chemical weapons as experienced during World War I led to widespread contempt for their use and culminated in the Geneva Protocol of 1925. It condemned the use of asphyxiating and poisonous gases but said nothing about the development or stockpiling of such weapons. Moreover, the United States did not ratify the Geneva Protocol until 1975.

Chemical weapons were not used in World War II and have never again been used by any major power in combat. Nevertheless, the quantity and sophistication of chemical weapons arsenals continued to grow, with new and more lethal agents, better delivery systems, and ultimately, the development of binary weapons that greatly reduced the risk to the troops using chemical weapons.[4] Biological weapons technology has also advanced, both for the weapons themselves and for delivery systems and agents. Traditional agents such as anthrax spores have become easier to manufacture, and more sophisticated agents of extraordinary toxicity have been developed. One of the earliest of these was botulinal toxin. By some estimates, for example, a single ounce (about 35 grams) of botulinal toxin can kill 60 million people.[5]

Military Disenchantment, Arms Control Success

By the late 1960s, the United States began to conclude that despite their great lethality, chemical and biological weapons (CBW) were of little military value. It is far too difficult to calculate the effect of biological weapons—in the worst case, they can be blown back onto the side that uses them. Chemicals can be targeted more precisely and have an immediate effect, but they are unlikely to be decisive against an enemy that takes reasonable protective measures (such as masks and suits). In the main scenarios for which the United States prepared during the Cold War, the enemy was presumed to be the Soviet Union, which had the capability to protect itself against chemicals. The United States nevertheless continued to maintain supplies of chemical weapons and planned for their use, but it did so primarily to ensure that an opponent (most likely the Soviet Union) would have to "suit up"—to prepare itself by wearing protective clothing and masks. If it were only American soldiers who had to wear hot, uncomfortable, and confining chemical protection suits in battle, they might well find themselves at a disadvantage.

When the United States ratified the Geneva Protocol in 1975, it renounced the use of chemical weapons. It had signed the Biological and Toxin Weapons Convention in 1972, after having unilaterally eliminated its biological weapons program a few years earlier. By the mid-1980s, new protective-suit technologies had emerged; they were lighter, cooler, and more flexible, promising to eliminate much of the disadvantage associated with having to be the only combatant to wear protective suits. Furthermore, after the Soviet Union came to an end and Russia was no longer an enemy, the risk of facing a Russian chemical attack, especially one using weapons kept in violation of international agreements, declined dramatically. Thus, the U.S. military dropped its long-standing opposition to the Chemical Weapons Convention. The CWC was signed in 1993 and ratified in 1997. Together, the BWC and CWC outlawed the development, storage, and use of biological and chemical weapons.

The BWC and CWC have reflected the decisions of all major powers that chemical and biological weapons do not constitute a promising method of warfare. Chemicals played their last decisive role in major warfare in World War I (although Saddam Hussein's Iraq used them with some effect against Iran in the 1980s), and biological weapons have never been used in modern war. The risk of a major conventional war escalating to an all-out nuclear exchange has made any war between the great powers improbable, but if there were a major conventional war, modern protective suits and other defenses make it unlikely that chemicals could be decisive. Biological weapons remain difficult to use on the battlefield, and anthrax vaccinations of military personnel make the most easily obtainable biological agent less effective each year. Finally, the very real possibility that a chemical or biological attack would provoke either an overwhelming conventional military response or in extremis a nuclear response remains a strong deterrent. Neither superpower gave up much usable military capability by agreeing to the BWC and later the CWC.

The New Threat of Chemical and Biological Weapons

Today's threat of chemical and biological weapons comes from rogue states—states that refuse to join the CWC or BWC, or that join and cheat—and from nonstate terrorist groups. Few notions within the U.S. national security and defense communities get as much attention as does the growing anxiety over a chemical or biological weapons attack on American citizens. Many foreign policy experts, both in and out of government, argue that the question is no longer "if," but "when" a chemical or biological weapon of mass destruction will be used against the United States or its allies. The secretary of defense has stated that a "race is on between our preparations and those of our adversaries."[6]

Despite the end of the Cold War, the threat of CBW remains serious for three reasons. First, the technology necessary to make and deliver chemical and biological weapons is now more widely available, better understood, and less expensive. Second, other sources of destructive power for many of the actors whose use of these weapons is feared have been increasingly closed off. Many of the states in question were able to purchase conventional weapons during the Cold War from the Soviet Union on favorable terms but have no other current affordable options. Third, America's overwhelming power and the spread of its influence have motivated the rise of opposition to it, some of which is based on religious ideology. Many such opponents see chemical and biological weapons as the only feasible and significant threat to the United States.

Saddam Hussein maintained a massive chemical and biological program, used chemicals against Iranian troops and against the Iraqi Kurds, and probably would have used them against Israel and coalition troops in the Persian Gulf War had the ground war been protracted. He chose not to preempt with chemical and biological weapons during the air war, partially because threats of nuclear retaliation deterred him, and partially because he thought he could wait out the air attack and did not want to unnecessarily provoke a ground attack. Once the ground war began, it was over before he could organize a chemical response, so it is impossible to know what his intentions might have been.

American military preponderance increases the chance that an attack on the United States will now come by nontraditional means. As one group of experts concluded, "The clear advantage of U.S. forces seems to suggest that potential adversaries would have learned the lesson [from the Gulf War] that to oppose the United States in conventional war would be futile; they would be more likely to employ asymmetric means to attack perceived weaknesses."[7] America's vulnerability is not its military strength, but its open society and porous borders, making it vulnerable to a chemical or biological attack against its cities.

Not only could a chemical attack on civilians kill tens of thousands and a biological attack potentially millions, any CBW attack would threaten important aspects of the American way of life. In the scramble to preclude any further CBW attacks, many civil liberties Americans take for granted would be limited or even revoked. Former secretary of defense William J. Perry has suggested this and recommended that to forestall such an outcome, the United States should "invent a new security structure from the ground up" that integrates national security agencies, domestic law enforcement, and emergency medical response capabilities to deal with the imminent threat. The new structure would have to walk a fine line between respecting civil liberties and maximizing a multilayered response to what Perry terms "catastrophic terrorism."[8]

Others argue that the risk of such an event is far less than the hype and suggest that the scare is self-perpetuating, building its own bureaucratic momentum. Some worry that excessive scare talk by government officials might itself lead to a significant cost to the American way of life and an unnecessary financial burden.[9] The recent report of the National Commission on Terrorism, which called for the monitoring of all foreign students, using criminals and terrorists as American spies, and making wiretapping easier, generated a reaction of this nature.[10]

The immediacy of the threat may be uncertain. The worst-case estimates of potential fatalities, such as predictions of millions of deaths from a biological weapons attack, assume a degree of weapons development capability and operational sophistication that would be difficult for terrorists or rogue states to obtain. But it is undeniable that many states and terrorist groups are attempting to develop or acquire CBW. In April 1999, a senior intelligence official responsible for nonproliferation, speaking on background, estimated that at least six-teen states have active chemical weapons programs and perhaps a dozen states are pursuing offensive biological weapons capabilities.

Dealing with CBW Attacks

Deterrence can be effective against states contemplating the development or use of CBW. Chapter 2 recommends that all weapons of mass destruction and their delivery systems, including CBW, be held at risk of nuclear attack in certain limited circumstances. Nuclear attack would be a last resort, but the threat of nuclear attack can add to the strength of CBW deterrence. There is evidence that it played a decisive role in deterring Saddam's use of CBW during the Gulf War. Most states can be deterred by maintaining overwhelming conventional military power and the will to use it. Few leaders would undertake a CBW attack if they were certain that the United States would spare no means in destroying their government and military forces in retaliation.

A terrorist attack is more difficult to deter than a state attack. If the perpetrator is a religious extremist group, its goal might be simply to kill as many Americans as possible without regard to any military benefit from the attack. Individuals involved in the attack might anticipate entering heaven as martyrs and thus have no concern for personal consequences. Unlike a state carrying out a military or quasi-military operation, a terrorist organization might believe it could slip away, offering no viable target for retaliation. Nevertheless, deterrence can still play a role in stopping terrorist attacks. Not all those involved are likely to relish the idea of dying for the cause of the group, and a significant attack is likely to require state support, which is subject to traditional deterrence. But since the effectiveness of deterrence against terrorists is uncertain, the only long-term solution is to dismantle terrorist organizations before they can carry out attacks.

The U.S. government has increased its domestic preparations and passive defenses to limit the damage a chemical and biological weapons attack might cause the civilian population.[11] One goal of these steps is to deter such an attack by reducing its potential effect. Suitable preparation can alleviate the consequences should an attack occur, but the lethality of chemical and biological weapons is such that if they are used against unprotected civilians, only a limited amount can be done to help most of the victims survive and recover. Most potential attackers know this. Only a much more extensive program to provide passive protection (protective suits and masks), detection equipment, and training to a significant proportion of the U.S. civilian population would be effective enough to convince a terrorist group determined to kill many Americans to give up a chemical or biological attack option. Such preparations were carried out in Israel during the 1991 Gulf War. They had a major impact on the morale of Israeli citizens and almost shut down the Israeli economy. But with Scud missiles landing in Tel Aviv, citizens accepted the need for them. Absent a much more visible and immediate threat to American cities, such extensive preparations seem unlikely to be acceptable in the United States.

Enforcing CBW Abolition

The CWC and BWC have the support of all the major powers. The objective of the international community should be to enlist every nation in the world to join both conventions. BWC support is nearly universal; Israel is the only major state that has not signed. Iraq, Libya, North Korea, and Syria are the key states who have not signed the CWC; all of these states were identified by Director of Central Intelligence George Tenet in March 2000 as countries that "now either possess or are actively pursuing" chemical weapons. Egypt has also refused to sign because of Israel's undeclared nuclear weapons program.[12] Egypt has signed the BWC and the NPT, thus foregoing both biological and nuclear weapons programs. Whether or not Egypt actually views chemical weapons as a serious way to balance Israel's nuclear program, it has held its participation in the CWC hostage to Israel's dismantling its nuclear program and joining the NPT. There will be no resolution to this standoff until a full Middle East peace settlement is in place. As an interim measure, the United States has attempted to obtain assurances from Egypt that it has no active chemical weapons program.

The second challenge is to get the states that are parties to the Chemical Weapons Convention and the Biological Weapons Convention to comply with their terms. The Cold War–era BWC was negotiated with no verification provisions because President Nixon realized that the convention could not be verified to the standards accepted at the time. At a minimum, adequate verification would require extensive on-site inspections, which neither superpower was prepared to accept. Nevertheless, the United States had little to lose by agreeing to a ban on biological weapons even if it were nonverifiable. The United States had already terminated its own biological weapons program, and there was a significant benefit to setting a strong norm against biological weapons. The norm would make it easier to punish violators if caught, and the United States would get credit for moral leadership in abandoning its own program and organizing the worldwide ban. Enforcement would be left to the international community or, in some cases, to strong-willed individual states or small coalitions.

The negotiation of the CWC began during the Cold War but after on-site inspections had been incorporated into nuclear treaties and were no longer taboo. As a result, the CWC does include strong verification provisions. They start with extensive reporting requirements monitored by a new international agency, the Office for the Prevention of Chemical Weapons. The reporting requirements include detailed declarations of weapons, programs, and facilities, including commercial facilities producing precursor and dual-use chemicals. The OPCW is charged with reviewing declarations and carrying out both planned and "challenge" inspections of facilities. Much effort was put into gaining the support of the chemical manufacturers, since the data-reporting and inspection procedures are a significant burden on the industry. Many companies initially worried about losing trade secrets through corrupt or incautious foreign inspectors. At some compromise to OPCW's effectiveness, these problems were largely overcome to the satisfaction of the industry, which supported ratification of the treaty. Nevertheless, Senator Jesse Helms has blocked the implementing legislation necessary to permit challenge inspections of U.S.-based facilities, so this key provision is not yet in effect.

Negotiations have been underway for some time to add an OPCW-like mechanism to the Biological Weapons Convention but have been difficult to conclude. The challenges of finding the very small facilities involved in biological weapons research and development remain as great as ever, and many observers are skeptical that effective verification is any more feasible today than it was when the convention was completed in 1972. Despite the skepticism, many have come to see establishing a biological weapons verification regime as inevitable. As a major advocate of biological weapons arms control has written,

The U.S. has long held that due to the relative ease with which biological and toxin weapons can be produced and hidden or destroyed, true verification is currently out of reach. Domestic studies have shown that many proposed verification measures are likely to be unproductive and may provide opportunities for compromising proprietary information. However, it seems inevitable that the United States must acquiesce to overwhelming international pressures to establish a verification regime. This acquiescence will result in the generation of a new degree of regulation for those using, or conducting studies of, micro-organisms and toxins.[13]

THE UNSCOM EXPERIENCE

The Office for the Prevention of Chemical Weapons is somewhat like a permanent version of UNSCOM, the United Nations Special Commission that was charged with verifying the removal of all WMD programs from Iraq after the 1991 Persian Gulf War. UNSCOM looked for contradictions in Iraqi declarations and documents, developed its own intelligence, and made heavy use of the intelligence resources of coalition nations, particularly the United States. Some weapons were destroyed by Saddam without protest. Others were undeclared but found and destroyed by UNSCOM, particularly after Saddam's son-in-law defected and subsequently disclosed the hidden location of numerous boxes of incriminating documents. Although the son-in-law was summarily executed by Saddam's thugs within hours of returning to Iraq, the documents were already in UNSCOM's hands and serving their purpose. They proved that Saddam's weapons disclosures had been far from complete. Perhaps more telling was that they also proved that UNSCOM had been incapable of finding Saddam's programs or weapons on its own.

UNSCOM operated with a large and highly trained international team against a relatively small nation that had recently been overwhelmingly defeated in war. UNSCOM could move throughout Iraq (although its movements were often delayed and diverted). The full intelligence capabilities of the coalition nations were heavily focused on finding Iraqi cheating. Even so, in the end, UNSCOM failed to find all of Saddam's weapons of mass destruction, production facilities, or delivery systems. Most dramatically, 20 missing Scud missiles, large items indeed, were never found.[14]

UNSCOM's experience demonstrates that even in the best of circumstances, a multinational inspection team cannot find hidden chemical or biological weapons, production facilities, or delivery systems. The OPCW will not be operating in circumstances nearly as favorable as UNSCOM had in Iraq. OPCW will receive intelligence help but nothing like the efforts concentrated on Iraq after the Gulf War, and it must operate worldwide using numerous languages. UNSCOM could recruit experts put forward by coalition countries for relatively short and often exciting assignments. It attracted some of the best technical experts in the world. OPCW employees are career international civil servants like all other U.N. and multinational civil servants.

A REALISTIC ROLE FOR THE OPCW

The OPCW will probably find a few anomalies in the reports of member states and point to those discoveries as evidence of its success. There is no chance that it will find any serious violations. An extensive analysis by Allan Krass in 1997 concluded,

> There are some risks associated with the CWC. Some states may simply refuse to join and will have to be deterred or prevented from acquiring chemical weapons by traditional diplomatic, economic, or military measures, or simply be allowed to have them. Experience with the nuclear NPT should allow no illusions about the risk. . . . The CWC will improve transparency and reduce some military risks, but it will not make the world safe from chemical weapons.[15]

Since states know that OPCW inspectors can be easily fooled, a state with no intention to comply knows it can hide behind clean compliance reports from the OPCW while continuing its active clandestine programs. No control or prevention regime will ever be perfect, but one hopes it will at least not enable cheating. For a state that has decided to develop weapons of mass destruction covertly, there is a great advantage to bursting on the scene with a finished program. It is much easier for a threatened country to destroy an early-stage program in the way the Israelis destroyed the Iraqi Osirak nuclear research reactor with a bombing attack in 1981. Fashioning a rational and effective enforcement regime for the CWC requires acknowledging both the motives states have to cheat and the impossibility of finding cheating with an inter-national monitoring organization.

An alternative approach to verification is to put more emphasis on the CWC provisions that place the responsibility of implementing the convention within a state's territory on the signatory. Article 4, paragraph 1, of the Chemical Weapons Convention states, "The provisions of this Article and the detailed procedures for its implementation shall apply to all chemical weapons owned or possessed by a State Party, or that are located in any place under its jurisdiction or control." The international community should not rely on international "verification police," who have little chance of finding either government-sponsored or terrorist cheating on the CWC. Instead, it can help member states' parties to develop the best possible internal monitoring and law enforcement capability to ensure compliance. This assistance might range from providing technical monitoring and testing equipment to training law enforcement officials and helping to organize specialized enforcement organizations. A state that obviously needs the assistance but refuses it would be ipso facto suspect. On the other hand, a state that accepts the assistance will of necessity have to open up its own CBW monitoring and enforcement, providing additional transparency that can assist in either unmasking a covert program or reassuring the international community that no state sponsored program is present.

The OPCW could then reorient its efforts, moving away from attempting to verify detailed compliance to reporting on the overall quality of a state's efforts to demonstrate that there are no prohibited activities, either state sponsored or criminal, within its borders. Today, much OPCW effort is expended looking for innocent and irrelevant discrepancies in the mountains of reports submitted by tens of thousands of facilities. OPCW should focus more on each state's internal system for obtaining and ensuring the accuracy of its reports, much like a corporate auditor focuses on the system for recording financial transactions rather than on the thousands of individual transactions. Such an audit would make it more difficult for a state to cover up a covert program. An overall audit report could be provided directly to the U.N. Security Council and include a general assessment of the WMD threat to the world's security as well as assessments of the actions of states that are parties to the three nonproliferation treaties.[16] A bad report would strongly pressure a state to accept outside assistance in improving its efforts. The outside assistance would either correct the weakness or provide more transparency into suspicious behavior.

This approach would be beneficial for improving compliance with all three nonproliferation regimes—the BWC, the CWC, and the NPT. Some have suggested merging the organizations carrying out the monitoring of the three treaties. There would be significant advantages to such a combination—pooling intelligence, building a better corps of trained inspectors and auditors, and clarifying the mission as being enforcement of the ban on all WMD proliferation.[17] Reorienting the focus to providing an audit of each state's own procedures rather than a "clean bill of health" would simplify the consolidation of WMD nonproliferation enforcement organizations.

PUNISHING NONCOMPLIANCE

States will continue to refuse to join the CBW conventions or will be caught cheating on the conventions' terms. There is no magic solution available to make them comply. In each case, an ad hoc combination of diplomatic, economic, and military actions must be formulated. The CWC itself incorporates the concept of diplomatic and economic measures in its Article 12, "Measures to Redress a Situation and to Ensure Compliance, including Sanctions." The treaty envisions "restricting or suspending the State Party's rights under this Convention" as well as what "collective measures" are to be taken in case of "serious damage to the object and purpose of this Convention" (i.e., problems with compliance and failure to rectify the situation within the specified time).[18] In each case the details have been left to be worked out, and the treaty does not automatically authorize military force, which will sometimes be necessary. The attack against Iraq's WMD facilities in 1998 after Saddam expelled UNSCOM inspectors is an example of what must be done when diplomacy and sanctions fail.

The challenge is for the United States to maintain enough priority on CWC and BWC compliance to achieve results. Doing so will be almost impossible if the effort is unilateral. Domestic support will always be hard to obtain, and other states will undercut the effectiveness of whatever actions are taken. Perhaps the most important change needed in America's approach to nonproliferation enforcement is to accept the essentiality of organizing coalitions to deal with proliferation. Without the cooperation of other nations, the United States will be left with either the frequent failure of its unilateral efforts to force compliance, or with the necessity of escalating military conflict as far as necessary to achieve the desired result.

Notes

1. Jessica Stern, *The Ultimate Terrorists* (Cambridge: Harvard University Press, 1999), p. 42.

2. Mike Iavarone, "Armory: Gas Warfare, Trenches on the Web," 1997, www.worldwar1.com/arm006.htm.

3. "Convention on the Prohibition of the Development, Production and Stockpiling of Bacteriological (Biological) and Toxin Weapons and on Their Destruction," fact sheet by the Arms Control and Disarmament Agency of the U.S. government, see www.acda.gov/treaties/bwc1.htm.

4. Binary chemical weapons consist of two separate chemical agents that become lethal only when they are combined during the use of the weapon.

5. Lord Lyell (general rapporteur), *Chemical and Biological Weapons: The Poor Man's Bomb,* North Atlantic Assembly, October 4, 1996.

6. William S. Cohen, "Preparing for a Grave New World," *Washington Post,* July 26, 1999.

7. Amos A. Jordan, William J. Taylor Jr., and Michael Mazarr, *American National Security* (Baltimore: Johns Hopkins University Press, 1999), p. 251.

8. Ashton Carter and William J. Perry, "A False Alarm (This Time): Preventive Defense against Catastrophic Terrorism," *Preventive Defense* (Washington, D.C.: Brookings Institution Press, 1997), pp. 143–74.

9. Ehud Sprinzak, "The Great Superterrorism Scare," *Foreign Policy* (Fall 1998), pp. 110–24; and Jonathan B. Tucker and Amy Sands, "An Unlikely Threat," *Bulletin of the Atomic Scientists* 55, no. 4 (July/August 1999).

10. See www.salonmag.com/news/feature/2000/06/12/terrorism.

11. Such preparations range from stockpiles of vaccines and gas masks to mobile task forces.

12. For a current list of nonsignatories of the conventions, see www.projects. sipri.se/cbw/docs.

13. "Science's Call to Arms: The Bacteriological (Biological) and Toxin Weapons Convention (BWC)," fact sheet from the Chemical and Biological Arms Control Institute, available at www.cbaci.org/cal2arms.htm.

14. Richard Butler, *The Greatest Threat* (New York: PublicAffairs, 2000).

15. Allen Krass, *The United States and Arms Control* (Westport, Conn.: Praeger, 1997), p. 127.

16. See McGeorge Bundy et al., *Occasional Report,* U.N. Association, May 1995, for a similar suggestion but with the responsibility for the report assigned to a special rapporteur to the Security Council rather than to the monitoring agencies.

17. Jessica Tuchman Mathews has developed this concept in unpublished writings.

18. Chemical Weapons Convention, September 16, 1999, see www.acda.gov/treaties/cwcart.htm#XII.

Chapter 6

Intelligence and Law Enforcement

Any successful effort to halt the proliferation of weapons of mass destruction must have good intelligence. Efforts by terrorists and rogue states can often be thwarted through diplomatic pressure, law enforcement operations, or military action if the nature, location, and organization of the activities are uncovered through intelligence operations. Often the WMD program must progress beyond the research phase to an actual effort to build weapons before it can be detected—Muammar Qaddafi's program to develop weapons of mass destruction, North Korea's nuclear program, and Iraq's twenty-year effort to develop nuclear weapons are all examples. In each of these cases, the program was detected and action taken before operational systems were fielded. Better intelligence could have led to earlier action, more satisfactory results, and lower costs, both in monetary and diplomatic terms.

Cold War Intelligence on Weapons of Mass Destruction

Past intelligence successes in uncovering proliferation efforts have resulted largely from superior technical intelligence, most of which was gathered and analyzed by the United States. The United States operates by far the largest intelligence system in the world. Most of the almost $30 billion it spends each year on intelligence goes to technical collection efforts: remote imagery, signals intelligence, and communications intelligence. The most effective intelligence technique against nuclear programs is satellite imagery, especially when supplemented with signals intelligence from missile flights and communications intelligence that tips off impending activity. Nuclear programs are big industrial operations, and each has a relatively large "signature" in satellite photographs. The weapons themselves must be tested at sites that have a unique configuration, and the missiles, bombers, and submarines needed to deliver them must be tested in the open. The large programs of Russia and China could not be hidden, and even the smaller programs of India and Pakistan were detected (though their details were not understood). Programs in Israel, South Africa, Argentina, Brazil, Taiwan, Iraq, Iran, and South Korea have also been detected, but since none of these countries has carried out overt tests of either nuclear weapons themselves or major delivery systems, much less can be learned about any of their programs from technical intelligence.

Today, the intelligence challenges are vastly different from those the United States faced when its main adversary was the Soviet Union. Technology is easy, sometimes trivial, to obtain. Computers capable of modeling nuclear explosives, once the subject of elaborate export controls, weigh three pounds and can be purchased anywhere. Biological and chemical weapons can be manufactured in one-room factories using off-the-shelf components. These activities can and must be found and stopped. But doing so requires techniques much more akin to those of law enforcement than to those of military intelligence. Satellite surveillance will play a secondary role. Espionage (informers) and communications intelligence (wiretaps) will have to bear a greater burden in this effort.

Communications Intelligence

Communications intelligence, by far today's most important area of technical intelligence in support of nonproliferation, is under a significant threat. A few years ago, unencrypted microwave or satellite links transmitted a significant portion of all communications. These forms of transmission could be intercepted by satellites or by judiciously placed ground stations. Today, by far the bulk of the world's communications is transmitted over fiber-optic lines that can be wiretapped only with extremely sophisticated covert operations, and much of what can be intercepted is encrypted.

Until the last five to ten years, unbreakable encryption was available only to the intelligence and military organizations of the world's most advanced powers. Three new technologies have emerged to make it available to anyone. The first technology is public key cryptography, invented in the 1970s, which solves the age-old cryptography problem of how to distribute a secret key among parties to an encrypted communication. Public key cryptography permits sending the secret keys safely over the same communication lines used for the encrypted message itself. The second technology is the fast microprocessor. Encrypting and decrypting messages require a significant amount of mathematical manipulation. But with current personal computers capable of a billion cycles per second, the time it takes to perform these manipulations is hardly noticeable—often less than a second even for a large message. The third technology is the Internet, which allows easy and anonymous connections throughout the world and has facilitated the distribution of often-free encryption technology. Netscape invented "secure sockets layer" public key encryption and included it in its free Internet browsers beginning in the mid-1990s. Microsoft later incorporated the technology into its Internet Explorer browser. The encryption included at no cost in these ubiquitous products is beyond the theoretical limits of what can be broken.

The Internet has also complicated communications intelligence in other ways. It has led to an explosion of communication volume, making it harder to sort out relevant messages from those with no intelligence interest. The Internet is largely anonymous—that is, it is not possible to know who is talking just by knowing the party's phone number. And finally, it transmits communications (including voice and even video) in trillions of disjointed data packets each day. "Tapping" at a particular point often will not even allow capture of all the packets of a particular conversation, since they can travel on many paths, only to be reassembled into a coherent stream at the destination.

There has been a major debate within the U.S. government in recent years over the security of the nation's communications infrastructure and of the Internet in particular. The proper role of encryption has been at the center of this debate. On one side are those who see nearly universal encryption of all communications as essential to the security of the Internet. Some of these advocates focus on the importance of encryption to ensuring individual privacy. Others focus on the threat that hackers and potential terrorists or even hostile governments pose to the nation's infrastructure. Hacking through to telephone switches, power system controls, air traffic controls, or financial institutions could wreak havoc with the nation's economy and even its military organizations. Only full encryption (and its byproduct of full authentication of the source of any communication) can eliminate these risks.

On the other side of the debate are the police, led by the FBI. Their dependence on effective wiretaps in attacking organized crime, drug cartels, and potential terrorists has been so great that they see encryption as a threat to the effectiveness of all U.S. law enforcement. Surprisingly, the National Security Agency (NSA), which is responsible for breaking the codes of military and diplomatic communications, has not taken a strong stand against the spread of encryption. A decade ago, the NSA supported legislation requiring all domestic encryption to be done with the Clipper Chip, a device that would give the U.S. government a "back door" to all private communications. The public outcry against the Clipper Chip was enormous, and Congress rejected the proposed legislation. Since then, the NSA has come to realize that the dramatic increase in the power of micro-processors and the speed of the Internet have made stopping the spread of encryption technology impossible.

There is a potential compromise solution that could help law enforcement organizations monitor the activities of terrorists and criminal organizations while providing strong protection against eavesdropping for private citizens and companies. Most financial activity on the Internet uses one of a small number of encryption technologies based on the implementation of secure sockets layer public key cryptography. It could be made a legal requirement that all commercial organizations make available to law enforcement, when operating with a court-issued warrant, the cryptographic keys necessary to de-scramble commercial messages. Since it is difficult for criminal or terrorist organizations to avoid using electronic commerce, at least some of their activities might be tracked in this way. Private noncommercial communications would not be subject to this requirement.

The technical, practical, civil liberties, and political challenges of implementing such a policy are enormous but not insuperable. If it were implemented, terrorists would know about it and attempt to avoid using any network services that could be intercepted. But criminals and terrorists know that conventional wiretaps are available to law enforcement and nevertheless find it impossible to avoid talking on open phone lines. Aggressive government-sponsored research and industry consultation should be undertaken to develop a reasonable design of a "key escrow" system limited to commercial transactions that would be available as a new law enforcement tool if other techniques of meeting terrorists threats prove inadequate.

Espionage and Cooperation

For the longer term, it would be a mistake to count on communications intelligence to play more than a supporting role in meeting the WMD threat. There will be little alternative but to return to old-fashioned espionage—human intelligence, or HUMINT as it is called in the intelligence community—to fill the gap left behind. The intelligence community has, by its own admission, allowed human intelligence capabilities to atrophy during its years of great success with technical intelligence. Restoring it will be a challenge.

Every effort, then, should be made to improve U.S. espionage programs. This requires recruiting more U.S. operatives, developing their foreign language skills, and improving their career prospects. The most productive approach to improve human intelligence is to organize effective cooperative arrangements with other intelligence services; U.S. overseas operatives should make these cooperative arrangements their first priority. There will be circumstances in which intelligence cooperation is not possible, and U.S. operatives will have to do the best they can to recruit agents. But the reality is that U.S. operatives will always have trouble recruiting and managing reliable agents capable of penetrating terrorist organizations. Much better results are likely to come from the law enforcement organizations of local governments that have penetrated terrorist organizations on their own soil.

Cooperation is inherently difficult in the intelligence world. If sources and methods cannot be protected, the sources will dry up. Creating good intelligence almost always involves the challenge of evaluating and fusing raw intelligence from many sources. To carry out the fusion effectively, the analysts must understand their sources and be able to evaluate them, deciding how much weight to give each. Developing a multinational cooperative approach to intelligence requires sharing sources and methods. The United States and the United Kingdom share virtually 100 percent of their intelligence, and significant sharing takes place with Canada and Australia. A substantial amount is shared with NATO and other allies as well. The trouble is that those countries with which the United States has traditionally shared intelligence do not have much better penetration of the terrorist groups and rogue states posing the main WMD terrorist threats than does the United States. An effective cooperative approach must develop effective sharing of intelligence with countries that have not historically been U.S. intelligence partners and that have not always been trustworthy.

One approach would be to organize a trusted third party to receive raw intelligence on WMD threats and terrorism, protect the sources and methods, analyze and integrate raw intelligence into finished analyses, and share the analyses with international organizations and other states. A trusted state widely considered to be politically neutral, such as New Zealand, Switzerland, or Sweden, could serve this function.

While the explosion of the Internet has made communications intelligence more difficult to carry out, the Internet could well facilitate a renaissance in espionage. The vast majority of counterintelligence successes against spies have come when the spy attempted to communicate with his or her handlers. In the past, this required physically transmitting documents. The Internet makes it possible to hide reports, pictures, maps, drawings, and any form of information in undetectable encrypted web traffic. Counterintelligence is not completely helpless against such techniques, but a clever spy can be much more comfortable than ever before in history that his or her "take" has gotten out undetected.

Cooperative Law Enforcement

The law enforcement organizations of the United States are inadequately equipped to deal with the growing threat of WMD proliferation. They are especially ill equipped to deal with matters requiring sophisticated international cooperation. They are disorganized, fractionated, underfunded, and not focused on the WMD threat. A good recent example of this situation was the June 26, 1996, Khobar Towers bombing in Saudi Arabia, which killed nineteen Americans. The incident was treated as an international law enforcement matter. The FBI director, Louis Freeh, was sent to Saudi Arabia to organize a joint effort. Perhaps Saudi Arabia was not capable of finding the perpetrators. What was nonetheless clear was that it was not possible to organize appropriate law enforcement cooperation between the United States and Saudi Arabia, two radically different societies, on a fast-response basis. Only if the law enforcement institutions had worked together over a period of years, with each country having experts in the system of the other country, could the operation have been a success.

There are also organizational problems within the U.S. government that must be solved if international law enforcement cooperation on WMD proliferation is to function as it must. To begin with, the traditional split of responsibilities between the CIA and FBI has already broken down in practice and should be reconsidered. Concern about the CIA spying on American citizens is legitimate—the disclosures of the 1970s made clear that presidents and directors of Central Intelligence were all too quick to misuse the intelligence community. But the reality is that intelligence and law enforcement must share technology, systems, targets, and analytical product if the threat of terrorism is to be met. Less of a "Chinese wall" between the agencies and greater spending on independent inspectors general to oversee activities that threaten civil rights are important reforms.

Every significant overseas counterterrorism and nonproliferation effort involves numerous federal agencies—the departments of State, Defense, Justice (including its quasi-independent FBI), Treasury (which includes the bureaus of Customs and of Alcohol, Tobacco, and Firearms), and the CIA. Coordination of these agencies has been only partially successful. For international operations to succeed, the United States has to speak with a single voice. To this end, each U.S. ambassador should have a senior "law enforcement cooperation officer" (LECO) as a member of the embassy country team with complete authority over all law enforcement and intelligence officers working on counterterrorism, counterproliferation, and counternarcotics. LECOs should receive special diplomatic, intelligence, and law enforcement training and be able to serve in this field for most of their careers.

The budget for federal law enforcement activities related to terrorism and proliferation has increased dramatically, from about $750 million in 1994 to $3 billion in 2000.[1] However, if the law enforcement agencies are asked to bear the chief responsibility for verifying and enforcing nonproliferation treaties within every country's borders, even greater increases will be needed. An additional $5 billion per year in U.S. law enforcement spending focused on weapons of mass destruction could be usefully spent. A significant portion of that increase should be used to provide training and equipment to other countries, thus facilitating the development of a worldwide cooperative law enforcement effort against the WMD threat. Meeting the new WMD threats will require not only increases in spending, but also innovation in budgeting procedures, congressional committee jurisdictions, and foreign aid administration. The current rigid bureaucratic and legislative barriers between domestic law enforcement, intelligence, defense, and foreign aid prohibit developing fully effective responses.

Note

1.   See www.salonmag.com/news/feature/2000/06/12/terrorism.

Chapter 7

Leadership and Consistency

The Indispensable Power

It has become a truism that the United States is the "indispensable power," that without American leadership no major world problem can be solved. Virtually no conceivable combination of powers can challenge America's conventional military might. The economic strength of the United States touches every corner of the earth. Its veto over almost every major multilateral institution means that no concerted action can be taken without America's agreement.

The challenge posed by the proliferation of weapons of mass destruction cannot be met without U.S. leadership. Yet recent American actions appear to other nations to presage America's withdrawal from this effort. The United States refused to join the Ottawa Convention on the Prohibition of Land Mines. Although not technically weapons of mass destruction, land mines are weapons that have caused thousands of injuries and the deaths of innocent children and civilian adults. The U.S. Senate refused to ratify the Comprehensive Test Ban Treaty, which was signed by all but a handful of states. The United States has not fully implemented the verification provisions of the Chemical Weapons Convention. The United States has not fully paid its U.N. dues.

When the United States decides to take an action, it often appears to be unilateral and arrogant. European companies are embargoed because they sell oil-related services to Iran; cruise missiles are sent against Osama bin Laden across the territory of sovereign states; a chemical plant in Sudan is destroyed as a result of less than definitive intelligence reports; an ABM system is planned to be deployed notwithstanding the opposition of virtually all other nations.

One explanation for what seems to many to be America's growing isolation and arrogance is the dominance of conservative Republicans, particularly Senator Jesse Helms, in the foreign policy leadership of the U.S. Senate. Senator Helms pushed aside the more moderate Richard Lugar as chair of the Senate Foreign Relations Committee after the Republicans gained control of the Senate in 1994. He has since blocked the CTBT, U.N. dues payments, and numerous Clinton administration foreign policy and national security personnel appointments. Some feel that the end of Senator Helms's career or the election of a Republican president with more control over members of his own party would restore America's international leadership, including leadership on matters related to weapons of mass destruction.

This view is vastly oversimplified. Senator Helms has fought effectively against many U.S. actions that would have furthered the cooperation policies of not only the Clinton administration but also of the Republican Reagan and Bush administrations that preceded it.[1] Yet he could not have succeeded in his efforts if there were not significant support for his position in both the Senate and the country at large. This support is largely a result of the failure of recent administrations to make a compelling case for the policies being implemented. Similarly, growing international opposition to U.S. programs is not a problem that can be solved without addressing America's failure to articulate and pursue consistent policies that can achieve widespread consensus.

No First Strike

The United States asserts that its nuclear policy is entirely defensive in nature and that nuclear weapons are kept strictly for deterrence. As explained in Chapter 2, however, the reality is otherwise. Under current strategy and planning guidance, U.S. "prompt retaliatory" war plans against Russia are de facto first-strike war plans. U.S. forces are capable of executing these plans and are therefore capable of executing a first strike against any lesser power. This capability still serves the Cold War missions of damage limiting and extended deterrence in Europe, necessary when the Soviet Union had both the ability and the ideological motive to launch a massive conventional invasion of Western Europe. Such an invasion posed the greatest risk of starting an escalation that could lead to a nuclear holocaust. The United States and NATO threatened to start a nuclear war if necessary to defend Europe not because such a move was likely to lead to victory but because the threat of nuclear response was considered necessary to deter a conventional war from starting in the first place. Conventional war had to be deterred because if it started, it would likely escalate to tactical nuclear war and then on to a nuclear holocaust. It was a complicated policy fraught with circularity and apparent contradictions, but it worked.

During the Cold War, this policy did not motivate worries about U.S. hegemony. The Soviet Union was able to mobilize its economy to support its vast war machine. Combined with the forces of the Warsaw Pact, the Soviet Union was a comparable military power (some even argued it was stronger than NATO). Furthermore, except for the few years when the Strategic Defense Initiative dominated U.S. military efforts, there was no concern about an American national missile defense. The ABM Treaty meant that there would be no active defense, without which a first-strike capability against an adversary with thousands of well-protected nuclear weapons is impossible.

Russian offensive nuclear capability is already significantly less than Soviet capability was at the height of the Cold War, and future reductions have been agreed upon through START. The

United States has also eliminated weapons but proposes to maintain a force of 2,500 accurate strategic nuclear warheads—1,000 to 1,500 more than Russia is likely to be able to maintain. At the same time, the United States is headed once again toward the deployment of a national missile defense. If expanded, the NMD could be capable of intercepting the warheads remaining after a U.S. first strike. Russia, China, and possibly other nations see these trends as leading to a classic first-strike capability for the United States in the not-too-distant future.

The principles of nuclear stability were discovered and consistently advocated by the United States throughout the Cold War. They have now been learned and accepted in Russia (and to a lesser extent in China). By these principles, America's strategy and program constitute a major threat in the eyes of Russia and China. The threat is not that the United States will launch a "bolt out of the blue" nuclear strike. There is no conceivable motive for such a strike, and even if there were such a motive no national missile defense can be foolproof: It could not protect American cities entirely from nuclear retaliation. Rather, the threat is that a plausible first-strike capability would give the United States true military dominance over any conceivable coalition of nations.

Nations worry, as they have throughout history, that such dominance as the United States enjoys can embolden a state to force its economic, cultural, and political systems on others. Although America has no such motive today, some American political leaders argue for just such an outcome. Some nations believe that they must allow for the possibility that these leaders might come to control U.S. policy. Further, nations will, as the United States does, be influenced principally by military capabilities rather than by articulated intentions. As a result, nations will oppose America's current nuclear strategy and any significant unilaterally deployed national missile defense as heading toward military dominance. They will attempt to offset American military power, whether they are small and weak nations, such as North Korea and Iran, or large and strong, such as China, France, and Russia. Weapons of mass destruction will often be seen as the only way to balance American military power and American influence more generally. France, for example, is not a military threat to America but nevertheless maintains its nuclear arsenal partially as a way to give itself an independence of action relative to the United States that it would not otherwise have. Likewise, India's nuclear weapons provide it with independence of action with respect to China and Pakistan as the United States moves toward reconciliation with China and continues to support Pakistan. Ideological states such as Iran or North Korea hope to use their possession of weapons of mass destruction to permit them to pursue ideological campaigns without provoking an American military response.[2]

The loose coalition of nations that is emerging to oppose America's national missile defense deployment and nuclear policies more generally will complicate efforts to control the spread of weapons of mass destruction. To stop this trend, the United States must change its nuclear posture to a purely defensive one, focused on deterrence. As explained in Chapter 2, this does not require an absolute no-first-use pledge. A few limited threats can be handled militarily only with nuclear first use. Maintaining such a capability helps to deter these situations from arising in the first place. A purely defensive posture does require a no-first-strike policy, changing war plans and restructuring nuclear offensive forces along the lines described in Chapter 2. These changes will not satisfy the nuclear abolitionists, but they should be adequate to permit the development of both a cooperative approach to national missile defense that would not spur an international reaction against the United States and a concerted multilateral program to attack WMD proliferation.

Strong Deterrence

The spread of technology has made it impossible for any power, including the United States, to detect, locate, destroy, or defend against every WMD program that hostile powers can undertake. Iraq and North Korea almost succeeded in completing secret nuclear weapons programs; they and others continue to try. For those powers that cannot master the technology or obtain the materials necessary to develop nuclear weapons, biological weapons will present an ever more attractive alternative. The spread of biotechnology makes such long-understood agents as anthrax easy to manufacture and offers ever-increasing numbers of exotic, new, and virulent pathogens. Chemical weapons can be made in the tens of thousands of industrial chemical plants that exist around the world. The law enforcement, intelligence, active defense, and arms control policies recommended in this book can ameliorate this threat. Nevertheless, deterrence through the threat of retaliation, including nuclear retaliation, will continue to be a necessary component of any effective response to this challenge. A massive conventional force response will always be the preferred response to a chemical or biological attack, but the threat of nuclear retaliation should not be abandoned.

Robust deterrence will also continue to be necessary to balance the nuclear forces of Russia and China. Neither state will give up these forces, and both will strive to deploy forces capable of penetrating any national missile defense the United States deploys. They will also be able to hold at risk American troops abroad and the cities of America's friends and allies that rely on extended deterrence as a substitute for their own nuclear programs. A direct nuclear attack on the United States by either Russia or China is only a remote possibility, no matter what the United States does with its own nuclear force. Yet without a robust deterrent, both Russia and China (and perhaps even other lesser nuclear powers) will find ways to leverage their nuclear power when their interests conflict with those of the United States.

The United States needs to be forthright about its reliance on nuclear deterrence as a major part of its defense against weapons of mass destruction, including its retention of limited nuclear first-use missions—notwithstanding the apparent conflict between retaining these missions and the limited no-first-use pledges the United States has accepted in conjunction with some arms control agreements. Ambiguity is an important element of effective diplomacy, especially in times of war or crisis when explicit policies or threats can be less effective than veiled ones. But ambiguity in strategy and overall policy leads to domestic political confusion and international uncertainty. The contradictions in WMD strategy that have arisen in the post–Cold War period have stood in the way of a consensus on how to deal with this growing threat. The gridlock induced by the decision to deploy a limited national missile defense against North Korea only brought these more fundamental contradictions to the surface.

A U.S. strategy of strong deterrence, including limited threats of nuclear first use, can nonetheless achieve wide acceptance as a nonthreatening defensive use of nuclear weapons. As compared with today's nuclear strategy and doctrine, it would permit a much greater reduction in America's total nuclear arsenal (to the 1,200 weapons advocated in Chapter 2)—a tangible manifestation of a move away from a threatening nuclear policy. In the United States, nuclear abolitionists will not be satisfied with such a strategy, particularly because it includes limited threats of nuclear first use. But a broad spectrum of foreign policy elites, senior military officers, and elected officials could nevertheless support such a policy. Overseas, NATO allies and other major nations will be pleased to see the change in policy and its accompanying reductions in America's nuclear force structure. NATO's official policy of "flexible response" will seem more anachronistic than ever, since it represents a potential first-use mission that will no longer be necessary.[3] No NATO member is likely to insist on a stronger nuclear capability than the remaining 200 air-launched U.S. weapons, British weapons, and the French *Force de Frappe*.

An explicit no-first-strike pledge, combined with force structure changes evidencing the policy change, will eventually ameliorate concern about a U.S. national missile defense. As discussed in Chapter 3, there are good reasons in any case for delaying a final decision to deploy a national missile defense. A reasonable delay might provide the time needed to develop a new cooperative approach to NMD, focused on the challenge of controlling the threat of weapons of mass destruction worldwide.

In principle, the necessary changes in U.S. offensive nuclear posture can be made in the context of START. The arms control gridlock described in this book, however, makes this unworkable. Domestic political pressure in favor of a limited ABM defense will probably continue, leaving only one or two years to settle these matters, even if the proposed system, which focuses on North Korea, is set aside. Furthermore, the U.S. Joint Chiefs of Staff will oppose reductions of nuclear weapons below 2,500 unless the planning guidance for the Single Integrated Operations Plan (SIOP) is changed.

A better path would be for the United States to exercise its leadership by announcing changes in nuclear strategy and force structure unilaterally, much as President Bush did when he withdrew land-based tactical nuclear weapons from all overseas deployments and began dismantling them. This step should break the deadlock. The Joint Chiefs of Staff could then certify that the proposed nuclear force structure is adequate to carry out national strategy. A proper restructuring of the ABM Treaty could be undertaken, in contrast to the approach attempted in 2000 that would have permitted only the initial phase, focused on North Korea, of the planned national missile defense.

Open Cooperation

The Nuclear Nonproliferation Treaty, the Chemical Weapons Convention, and the Biological Weapons Convention have provided a strong basis for international cooperation against the spread of weapons of mass destruction. They set the norm against any chemical or biological weapons since the CWC and BWC ban chemical and biological weapons altogether. The NPT recognizes five nuclear states but bans nuclear weapons for all others and commits all member states to work against proliferation.

These treaties are supported by a variety of multilateral institutions and other agreements. The Zangger Committee, the Nuclear

Suppliers Group, and the Wassenaar Agreement, for example, define nuclear weapons–related technologies subject to export controls; the Missile Technology Control Regime controls ballistic missile technology with the potential of supporting WMD attacks; and the Office for the Prevention of Chemical Weapons monitors compliance with the CWC.

These multilateral treaties and institutions are the product of long negotiations and much work to organize them. When they have found noncompliance, they have served an important political role in making it more difficult for the international community to ignore the situation. The treaties and their associated implementing institutions, however, cannot stop the slow and steady spread of weapons of mass destruction and the inevitable conflagration this spread will bring about. There are too many problems with an approach that relies too heavily on international "verification police" to ensure compliance with arms control treaties. There is strong evidence that a better approach is needed: The International Atomic Energy Agency has failed to uncover either Iraqi or North Korean nuclear programs; finding hidden chemical and biological production is a hopeless challenge; the conflict between intrusive international arms control verification and legitimate concerns over corporate trade secrets has kept the United States from full participation in the OPCW; and UNSCOM was unable to verify Saddam Hussein's compliance with Iraq's disarmament commitments.

Realism is needed in arms control implementation. During the Cold War, it became a truism that near-perfect verification was required for an arms control agreement to be successful. For treaties where un-detected cheating could mean defeat in war or a nuclear confrontation, this remains a good principle. It is not clear, however, that in the present world political climate there either is or can be such agreements. Rather, the main benefit of arms control in the post–Cold War era is the setting of basic rules. The enforcement arms of the main nonproliferation treaties—the NPT, the BWC (if one is negotiated), and the

CWC—will make a much better contribution if they monitor the quality of the effort being made by each member state to enforce the treaty within its own borders, rather than attempting to verify directly the terms of the treaties.

Much greater cooperation on intelligence and law enforcement is essential. New institutions are necessary to accomplish this cooperation, such as those suggested in Chapter 6. Existing multilateral intelligence and law enforcement institutions cannot succeed without access to the capabilities of the major nations, especially to those of the United States. At the same time, without international cooperation, the United States will find itself increasingly unable to carry out necessary human intelligence operations and to bring to justice international criminals trafficking in WMD technologies, delivery systems, and the weapons themselves.

The United States must also increase its efforts to organize ad hoc coalitions that support diplomatic pressure, sanctions, isolation, and military action against states that have refused to join the international conventions against WMD proliferation. These states include both those that the U.S. Department of State now calls "states of concern" (previously called "rogue states") as well as those in the special category—India, Israel, and Pakistan, the three de facto nuclear states—that are not permitted into the NPT.

The United States can use military action unilaterally when its vital interests are threatened, but only multilateral coalitions can be effective in applying diplomatic pressure and sanctions. By definition, only a multilateral coalition can enforce the isolation of a state. The United States should, as a matter of policy, drop most efforts to impose unilateral sanctions. The president should be given broad new authority to impose sanctions as coalitions are developed, but he should be relieved of the necessity of maintaining numerous legislatively mandated unilateral sanctions. Many of these are ineffective, and they interfere with the flexibility the president needs to organize effective coalitions and negotiate improved compliance from offending states.

Five nations need continuing special efforts directed toward them if the United States is to develop more effective cooperation on controlling the spread of weapons of mass destruction. The changes in U.S. policies and programs that this book recommends will provide an opportunity for a vigorous new approach toward each of these five nations:

- *Russia:* Dropping "prompt retaliatory" war plans and the first-strike capabilities they require should permit the completion of a STRANSS treaty and a reinvigoration of the Cooperative Threat Reduction program. CTR should be expanded to include much more law enforcement and intelligence cooperation. Russia needs a proper export control system to stop the flow of WMD technology, and the United States should offer more help to build it. In return, Russia can make available its considerable intelligence capabilities to help the international community in countering WMD proliferation.

- *China:* Intensive diplomacy will be needed to persuade China to accept the deployment of ballistic missile defenses—both theater missile defense and national missile defense—as elements of a revised American WMD strategy. The United States must tolerate China's modernization of its nuclear deterrent force if it expects China to accept an American NMD capable of destroying up to fifty warheads. In turn, China must accept the defensive nature of the American NMD and limit its own ballistic missile buildup, especially the buildup that threatens Japan, Korea, and Taiwan. By developing a new generation of sea-based TMD that could be used to help protect any of these nations, the United States can provide adequate support to its allies without the confrontation with China that land-based American-supplied TMD would engender.

- *Pakistan:* The first step in any effective WMD cooperation with Pakistan must be acceptance of the reality of Pakistan's circumstances and politics. Pakistan will remain nuclear as long as India is nuclear, and India will remain nuclear as long as China is nuclear, which will be a long time and maybe forever. Pakistan has yet to develop stable democratic institutions. It is at risk of becoming a failed state under the control of religious extremists. The policy of pressure, sanctions, financial punishment, and military isolation of recent years will fail. Pakistan must make many changes in order to deserve major U.S. assistance and protection. Pakistan's present leadership, however, seems capable of developing a regime of cooperation that might benefit both Pakistan and the United States.

- *India:* As with Pakistan, acceptance of reality must be the first step in developing cooperative relations with India. India has not been a major source of WMD proliferation beyond its own indigenous efforts to develop a nuclear deterrent. India has also done much less than is possible to help solve the WMD problem, however. The United States should attempt a grand bargain with India. India should be offered entry into the club of great powers, including permanent membership in the U.N. Security Council and admission to the NPT as a nuclear weapons state (perhaps with special provisions). In return, India would reach a settlement with Pakistan on Kashmir, accept limits on its nuclear program, and cooperate fully in the fight against WMD proliferation.

- *France:* France remains America's oldest ally, the source of much of U.S. culture and values, and a permanent member of the U.N. Security Council. It is the state that produced Cardinal Richelieu and the theory of a balance of power that motivates so much of its foreign policy. France will not abandon its devotion to these principles. The United States would be acknowledging the importance of those principles and responding to many French criticisms by making the changes recommended here. In that context, it should be possible to enlist France in a much more cooperative program than currently exists to sanction, isolate, and even attack states that refuse to accept international norms for WMD.

In addition to these nations of special concern, the United States should significantly increase its consultation with its chief allies, NATO and Japan, on matters related to weapons of mass destruction. Without their support for America's strategy, policies, and programs, it will be impossible to develop the coalitions necessary for success.

These many diplomatic initiatives require that significant new financial resources be devoted to American diplomacy. The main impediment to obtaining these resources has been Senator Helms. The policy changes proposed here, however, especially the incorporation of a national missile defense into U.S. national security strategy and the replacement of START and the ABM Treaty with a STRANSS treaty, should answer many of Senator Helms's long-standing criticisms of, and frustrations with, American foreign policy.

The new president should propose an increase of $5 billion per year to support new initiatives in intelligence, diplomatic operations, and foreign assistance directed at the problem of weapons of mass destruction. This is a small cost compared with the Department of Defense budget already devoted to defending the nation against weapons of mass destruction and a trivial cost compared with what would result from an actual WMD incident of almost any type.

Power and Leadership

The world we live in is a complex, co-evolving adaptive system. It will not remain static while the world's only remaining superpower adds to its military dominance, deploys a national missile defense while maintaining a de facto first-strike offensive force, and abandons arms control agreements once thought to be the cornerstone of strategic nuclear stability. Unless the United States adopts policies and programs that take into account the inevitability of other nations coalescing to oppose its absolute military dominance—no matter how benign they may see its current motives—the world will continue to become a less safe place. WMD proliferation will accelerate, both to rogue states and to terrorist groups. Some day, someone will use a nuclear bomb or mount a biological attack. Millions will be killed, and many institutions we hold dear will be gravely threatened.

The rationale behind the proposed national missile defense deployment against North Korea is not wrong. Rogue states should be met with whatever active defenses are possible. But the technology is far from complete, the national strategy into which the NMD is being shoehorned is inconsistent, and the diplomatic efforts to prepare the way have failed.

This book has proposed a strategic vision of strong deterrence coupled with open international cooperation around which the new president can organize a U.S. policy toward weapons of mass destruction that will achieve wide support domestically and internationally. The United States can and should use its moral, economic, and military power, not to dominate the world, but to lead the nations of the world in a fight against extremism, terrorism, and anarchy, toward the shared values of democracy, human rights, and freedom.

Notes

1. Senator Helms has supported some arms control agreements, voting for START, the CWC (although opposing aspects of CWC implementation), and the Conventional Forces in Europe flank agreement.

2. Some have argued that a primary motivation for nuclear proliferation is pride and the desire to obtain a more important "seat at the table" in international affairs. This is certainly one motivation, but

if the seat at the table is to have any value, it must be used in the pursuit of national interests as new nuclear states see them.

3. At some point in the not-too-distant future, NATO will need to adapt its flexible response nuclear policy. But the policy itself is flexible enough to accommodate the changes recommended in this book, and it would be difficult to change the policy until a broader consensus on nuclear strategy (including ballistic missile defenses) is obtained.

Index

About the Author

Jan Lodal served as principal deputy under secretary of defense for policy for four years of the Clinton administration. During the Nixon and Ford administrations, he served on the National Security Council staff as deputy for program analysis to Secretary of State Henry A. Kissinger. In both of these positions, he was deeply involved with the nation's nuclear policies and programs, as well with issues of weapons of mass destruction and defense policy more generally. He personally participated in three U.S.-U.S.S.R. summit meetings and several post–Cold War U.S.-Russia summits.

Mr. Lodal has been a member of the faculty of Princeton University and served as the director of the Aspen Strategy Group. He is a director of the Atlantic Council and a member of the Council on Foreign Relations, the American Economic Association, and the International Institute for Strategic Studies. In his business career, Mr. Lodal has focused on information technology, cofounding American Management Systems and founding two other software firms.

Jan Lodal is the recipient of Rice University's Distinguished Alumnus Award (for public service and achievement in business), the Defense Intelligence Agency's Director's Medal, and the Department of Defense Medal for Distinguished Public Service (awarded twice), the Department of Defense's highest civilian award. He has published numerous articles on defense policy, national security strategy, and arms control.